WORLD KITCHEN
INDIA

WORLD KITCHEN
INDIA

MURDOCH BOOKS

Contents

INDIA IS A VERY COMPLEX COUNTRY CULTURALLY, GEOGRAPHICALLY AND FROM A CULINARY POINT OF VIEW. COOKING STYLES VARY NOT ONLY FROM STATE TO STATE AND TOWN TO TOWN BUT ALSO FROM SUBURB TO SUBURB.

Modern India is one of the most diverse countries in the world. It is made up of 25 states and seven territories and its people use 18 major (and over 1600 minor) languages and practise seven major religions. Despite this, and its history of invasion and change, India has kept a strong sense of national identity and has used outside influences to its advantage.

INFLUENCES

Indian cuisine has had many influences, one of the biggest being vegetarianism, brought about by religious beliefs. Buddhism and Jainism came to India around the 6th century BC and though they faded as major religions in India, they were particularly successful in converting people to a way of life in which living beings are considered sacred. Hinduism predated both these religions but early Hindu texts such as the Mahabharata show that meat was not originally prohibited. Meat is still occasionally eaten by some Hindus. Over time, vegetarianism slowly pervaded Indian culture and today it is practised by many people, particularly in the South. The sacred status of the cow, a Vedic idea from before Hinduism, remains to this day.

In 1525, the Moghul emperors arrived and brought with them their own style of cooking, architecture and living, which affirmed their religion, Islam, and its Arabic heritage. Muslims had periodically been invading India since the 10th century but this later time was the period of their greatest influence. Pork was taboo but meats such as lamb and chicken were permitted as long as they were killed according to Muslim law. Many dishes were a product of the court chefs, who were trained in Central Asian, Persian and Afghani culinary styles. Money was no object and imagination was boundless. The Moghuls incorporated some of their favourite foods into Indian cuisine, such as almonds, cream and dried fruits. They also introduced cold weather fruit such as peaches, cherries and apricots to the orchards of Kashmir. The use of saffron and gold and silver leaf reflects the opulence of Moghul cuisine, especially in sweets. These influences are most apparent in northern India and in areas such as Hyderabad, the site of an ancient court, where there were Muslim settlements.

China had also long had an association with India via its maritime and overland trading routes. The karhai and wok are extremely similar in appearance, though which came first is impossible to say.

Influences from further afield can be seen in Goa and Kerala where the Portuguese established ports, in Chennai (Madras) where the British set up the East India Company, in Pondicherry, a French enclave, and in Kolkata (Calcutta), the centre of the British Raj. With the Europeans came more widespread Christianity and new styles of cooking to add to the established Muslim and Hindu ways. Foods imported from the New World via Europe, such as tomatoes, capsicums (peppers), chillies and potatoes, were gradually incorporated into local cuisines until in some cases, as with the chilli, they became ubiquitous.

The British influence on Indian cuisine was much less than the Indian impact on British food. The British encouraged the idea of frequently nibbling on tiffin, which are little snacks. The Indian cooks of the British Empire learned to make yeasted

bread, cakes and 'curries', which were more suited to the British palate. The British developed a liking for spicy food and transported the idea back home.

INDIAN FOOD MYTHS
The type of Indian food found in the majority of Indian restaurants is based on a successful menu formula. The original versions of these restaurants were run by Punjabis in India where they served a mixture of Punjabi cuisine, such as tandoori, and Moghul dishes such as korma and biryani. This menu represents a tiny section of Indian cuisine.

In India, there is no such thing as a curry. The word is of English origin, based on the Tamil word 'kari' meaning black pepper, and is used to denote all kinds of Indian dishes. Dishes in India are named for the combination of spices used (rogan josh), for the cooking method (korma, biryani, do piaza), or for their main ingredients (saag, aloo gobi). Curry powder does not exist within India; the closest equivalent is masala (spice mix). There are hundreds of masala combinations. In northern India, they tend to be dry mixtures using ground spices, such as garam masala, and in the southern areas, wet ones, such as coconut masala, using fresh spices.

EATING
Meat or vegetarian dishes are never the main part of the meal, but are an accompaniment to rice or breads and eaten alongside relishes, chutneys and other dishes such as dal. Yoghurt or curd is also served with meals and is useful for cooling hot or spicy food. The types of dishes vary according to religious group. Hindus tend to eat vegetable dishes and dals with boiled rice. Muslims serve meat and seafood dishes, breads, and fried snacks such as samosas, but dal does not play such an important part. Generally, Indian meals consist of a couple of vegetable dishes (and meat or fish where appropriate), some relishes or chutneys, yoghurt, rice, breads and a dessert, usually all served at once.

Meals are often served on thalis, which are large, flat plates, made from banana leaves or metal. The leaf or plate is covered with either small mounds

of food or with metal bowls called katoris which hold the food. The food, eaten with the fingertips of the right hand, is replenished as you eat.

Paan is a collection of spices and aromatics often served at the end of the meal to freshen the breath and act as a digestive. A betel leaf is folded around pieces of betel nut, and either lime paste, red katha paste, chewing tobacco or mitha masala (spices). The whole lot is chewed before being either spat out, or in the case of mitha masala, swallowed.

THE FOOD OF THE NORTH

The cuisines in the North cover a wide range of styles, the main influences being from the Moghuls and Punjabs, as well as the land, which produces a diverse range of grains. Traditionally, rice was not eaten in large quantities as it could not be easily grown. However, in Jammu and Kashmir, and also in Dera Dun, rice is now grown on the Himalayan foothills. Basmati, the king of rices, comes from Dera Dun and is prized throughout India.

As breads are a staple, there is a huge range to choose from. In Kashmir and Jammu, the kulcha and sheermal are Middle Eastern in style, in the Punjab and Haryana, naan are cooked in tandoors, and parathas, puris, chapatis and roti are widely eaten. Breads are usually served with dishes which have a thick sauce that is easily scooped up.

Dairy products such as malai (cream), paneer and yoghurt appear at almost every meal. Butter appears in the form of ghee or makhan (white butter). Dishes are thickened and enriched with cream and in the Punjab butter is used both as a condiment and as a flavouring. Rajasthani cuisine contains many dishes cooked in buttermilk, milk or butter.

Meat is a feature of northern cuisine, a reflection of Moghul influences as well as the Parsis and Sikhs. Lamb is popular though game is also favoured in the Punjab and Rajasthan. Pulses and legumes are commonly eaten and dal will accompany every meal.

Spices in these areas are based on 'hot mixes'. This means warmly flavoured spices rather than heat from chillies. The most well known is garam masala.

The custom of cooking in community ovens or tandoors prevails in rural areas, especially in the Punjab. The ovens are used to cook breads and roast meats, which is not possible in home-style kitchens, where pots are set above open fires.

THE FOOD OF THE CENTRE

Central India has an eclectic mix of foods that can be divided into East (Bengal), West (Gujarat and Maharashtra) and Central (Hyderabad) styles. Fish feature heavily on the coasts while Hyderabad has a cuisine with Moghul overtones, rich in meat.

Hyderabad uses southern aromatics and spices, such as tamarind and curry leaves, blended with a Moghul style of cooking.

Spices are varied in their use. Cumin, coriander, turmeric and chillies grow in Gujarat. These are all used extensively in the mainly vegetarian cuisine of the area. In Bengal, a spice mix called panch phoron dominates and mustard seeds and mustard oil are a common combination. Hyderabad uses southern aromatics and spices, such as tamarind and curry leaves, blended with a Moghul style of cooking.

Rice is a staple across most of the Centre. Red patni rice, with its chewy texture and nutty aroma, grows in the Centre and West. In Hyderabad, rice is cooked with saffron and spices for biryani and pulao, or added to lentils to make khichhari.

Dairy-based sweets such as rossogollas, gulab jamun and sandesh are found all over Bengal but especially in the capital, Kolkata (Calcutta).

Tea is grown all along the Brahmaputra valley in Assam, the main tea-producing area of India. It is here that the first tea gardens were established by the British in the 19th century. India's finest tea, however, is grown in Darjeeling in West Bengal.

THE FOOD OF THE SOUTH

The food of southern India has a lighter, fresher flavour than that of the northern parts. It is often more pungent due to its use of chillies and souring agents such as lime juice, kokum and tamarind. Freshly grated coconut is used in abundance and coconut milk is a common cooking liquid.

Along the west coast in Goa, Karnataka and Kerala, there are culinary influences from the Jews of Kochi (Cochin), the Syrian Christians, and the Portuguese. Commercial coconut cultivation was encouraged by the Portuguese, tea was planted by the British, and coffee, a legacy of Arab merchants, is more popular than tea. The chilli, which was to have a profound effect on the cuisine of India, arrived in Kerala with the Portuguese.

The spice centre of India is Kochi (Cochin) in Kerala and it is here that the Indian Spices Board has its headquarters. Cardamom, turmeric, vanilla, pepper and ginger grow in abundance and are sold locally and internationally via Kochi's spice market.

Rice is the main staple, along with pulses and legumes, and dishes are flavoured with wet (fresh) spice and herb mixtures, and coconut. Many dishes are tempered with a final seasoning (tarka), usually a combination of mustard seeds, dried chillies and curry leaves heated in oil and stirred into the dish. Pulses are eaten as dals and also ground into flours to make poppadoms and other deep-fried snacks. Appams, idlis and dosas are all common and are eaten with chutneys and stew-like dishes, or in the case of the dosa, holding a spicy potato filling.

Pork and beef are both eaten in Goa and Kerala, supported by a high level of religious tolerance. Vindaloo and bafath are popular pork dishes with European styles of cooking using local ingredients. Lamb is eaten by the Mappilas, the Muslims of the Malabar coast, descendants of Arab traders. Moghul-style recipes such as korma are cooked using southern flavours including coconut and curry leaves. In contrast, Karnataka and Tamil Nadu have a vegetarian bent to their cuisine.

Both the coast and waterways of the area provide many types of fish and shellfish. Seafood caught off the coast is some of the best in India.

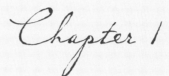

Chapter 1

TIFFIN

◇◇◇◇◇◇◇◇◇◇◇◇◇◇◇◇◇◇◇◇◇◇◇◇◇◇◇◇◇◇◇◇

Tiffin are a legacy of the British, who encouraged the custom of nibbling on little snacks – golden samosas, pakoras and bhajis, as well as soups, kofta and tikka.

Samosas

These crisp, deep-fried pastries are the most popular savoury snack in India. This recipe has a delicious spicy vegetable filling. Samosas are traditionally served with a chutney.

PASTRY
450 g (1 lb) maida or plain (all-purpose) flour
1 teaspoon salt
4 tablespoons oil or ghee

FILLING
400 g (14 oz) potatoes, cut into quarters
80 g (3 oz/½ cup) peas
1½ teaspoons cumin seeds
½ teaspoon coriander seeds

2 tablespoons oil
½ onion, finely chopped
¼ teaspoon ground turmeric
½ teaspoon garam masala (page 240)
2 green chillies, chopped
3 cm (1¼ in) piece of ginger, chopped
2 tablespoons chopped coriander (cilantro) leaves
1½ tablespoons lemon juice

oil, for deep-frying

To make the pastry, sift the maida and salt into a bowl, then rub in the oil or ghee until the mixture resembles breadcrumbs. Add 185 ml (6 fl oz/¾ cup) warm water, a little at a time, to make a pliable dough. Knead the dough on a floured surface for 5 minutes, or until smooth. Cover and set aside for 15 minutes. Don't refrigerate the dough or the oil will harden.

To make the filling, cook the potato in simmering water for 10 minutes, or until tender. Drain and cut into small cubes. Cook the peas in simmering water for 2 minutes. Drain and refresh them in cold water.

Place a small frying pan over low heat and dry-roast the cumin seeds until aromatic, then remove. Dry-roast the coriander seeds. Grind ½ teaspoon of the cumin and all the coriander to a fine powder in a spice grinder or pestle and mortar.

Heat the oil in a heavy-based saucepan over low heat and fry the onion until light brown. Stir in all of the cumin, the coriander, turmeric and garam masala. Add the potato, peas, chilli and ginger and stir for 1 minute. Mix in the coriander leaves, lemon juice and salt, to taste, then leave to cool.

On a floured surface, roll out a third of the pastry to a 28 cm (11 in) circle, about 3 mm (⅛ in) thick. Cut 10 circles with an 8 cm (3 in) cutter and spoon ½ tablespoon of filling onto the centre of each. Moisten the edges with water, then fold over and seal with a fork into a semicircle. Repeat to use all the filling and pastry. Cover until ready to fry.

Fill a karhai or a heavy-based saucepan one-third full with oil and heat to 180°C (350°F), or until a cube of bread browns in 15 seconds. Fry a few samosas at a time until lightly browned on one side, then turn over and cook until lightly browned on the other side. Drain the samosas on a wire rack for 5 minutes before draining on paper towels. Serve warm or cold.

MAKES 30

BHEL PURI

Bhel puri is a mixture of savoury morsels including crisp puffed rice, potatoes and green mango, tossed with tamarind chutney and mint chutney. Served freshly made in bowls, it is a favourite snack at sunset on Chowpatty beach in Mumbai (Bombay).

MINT CHUTNEY
50 g (2 oz/1²/₃ cups) coriander (cilantro) leaves
50 g (2 oz/2½ cups) mint leaves
6 garlic cloves, chopped
3 red chillies, chopped
½ red onion, chopped
3 tablespoons lemon juice

TAMARIND CHUTNEY
60 g (2 oz) fennel seeds
440 ml (15 fl oz/1¾ cups) tamarind purée (page 246)
100 g (4 oz) ginger, sliced
300 g (11 oz/1²/₃ cups) jaggery or soft brown sugar
1 teaspoon chilli powder
1 tablespoon ground cumin

1 tablespoon chaat masala (page 240)
1 teaspoon black salt

3 potatoes
1 tomato
120 g (4 oz) puffed rice
60 g (2 oz) sev (besan flour) noodles
1 green unripe mango, sliced into thin slivers
1 onion, finely chopped
4 tablespoons finely chopped coriander (cilantro)
   or mint leaves
1 teaspoon chaat masala (page 240)
12 crushed puri crisps (page 175)
coriander (cilantro) leaves

To make the mint chutney, blend the ingredients together in a food processor or pestle and mortar. Transfer to a saucepan and then bring to the boil. Remove from the heat, leave to cool, then season with salt. Set aside.

To make the tamarind chutney, put a small frying pan over low heat and dry-roast the fennel until aromatic. Mix together the tamarind, ginger, sugar and 250 ml (9 fl oz/1 cup) water in a saucepan. Cook over low heat until the tamarind blends into the mixture and the sugar has completely dissolved.

Strain out the ginger slices and cook the remaining mixture to a thick pulp. Stir in the fennel seeds, chilli powder, cumin, chaat masala and black salt. Season with salt and reduce, stirring occasionally, over medium heat until thickened to a dropping consistency (it will fall in sheets off the spoon). Leave to cool.

Cook the potatoes in boiling water for 10 minutes, or until tender, then cut into small cubes. Score a cross in the top of the tomato. Plunge into boiling water for 20 seconds, then drain and peel. Roughly chop the tomato, discarding the core and seeds and reserving any juice.

Put the puffed rice, noodles, green mango, onion, chopped coriander, chaat masala and puri crisps in a large bowl and toss them together. When well mixed, stir in a little of each of the chutneys. Vary the chutney amounts depending on the flavour you want to achieve. The tamarind chutney has a tart flavour and the mint chutney is hot. Serve in small bowls and garnish with coriander leaves.

Leftover mint chutney can be eaten with samosas (page 16) or pakoras (page 32) but it cannot be stored. Refrigerate unused tamarind chutney in a jar for several weeks.

SERVES 6

Lamb Kofta

These miniature meatballs are often served as a snack in homes and restaurants. They are a typical example of a dish that migrated from Persia to India. The meatballs are succulent inside because the mixture is thoroughly kneaded before cooking.

1 small onion, roughly chopped
5 cm (2 in) piece of ginger, roughly chopped
2 garlic cloves, roughly chopped
2 green chillies, seeded and roughly chopped
15 g (½ oz/½ cup) coriander (cilantro) leaves
2 tablespoons thick plain yoghurt (page 246)
500 g (1 lb 2 oz) minced (ground) lamb

2½ teaspoons ground cumin
1½ teaspoons ground coriander
2 teaspoons garam masala (page 240)
¼ teaspoon chilli powder
2½ teaspoons salt
½ teaspoon ground black pepper
3–4 tablespoons oil

Blend the onion, ginger, garlic, chopped chilli and coriander leaves in a food processor until they form a paste. Alternatively, use a pestle and mortar, or finely chop everything together with a knife. Add the yoghurt to the paste and mix well.

Put the lamb in a bowl, add the paste and mix by hand, kneading the ingredients into the meat until thoroughly combined. Add all the spices, and the salt and pepper, and mix again to distribute evenly. Cover and refrigerate for 1–2 hours to allow the flavours to develop and also to make the mixture firmer and therefore easier to handle.

Wet your hands and roll small handfuls (about a heaped tablespoon) of the mince mixture into balls. You should have about 30–40 meatballs.

Heat 1 tablespoon of the oil in a large, heavy-based frying pan. When the oil is hot but not smoking, add 10 meatballs in a single layer. Brown all over by gently shaking the pan for 2–3 minutes. Don't be tempted to turn them over with a spoon or they may break up. Test a kofta by breaking it open. If the meat is still pink, cook for another minute or two. Remove and drain on paper towels. Repeat with the remaining meatballs.

Serve the meatballs with cocktail sticks for picking them up. Mint and coriander (cilantro) chutney (page 211) is the perfect accompaniment but other chutneys are also suitable.

SERVES 6

CHUCUMBER

A very healthy snack from north India often served as a starter in restaurants, or with drinks. Many of the ingredients can be increased or decreased according to personal taste. The combination of cucumber and fresh coriander is very refreshing.

1 red onion, finely chopped
2 small cucumbers, about 200 g (7 oz), finely chopped
100 g (4 oz) ripe tomatoes, finely chopped
3 tablespoons finely chopped coriander (cilantro)
1 red chilli, finely chopped
1 green chilli, finely chopped

1½ tablespoons lemon juice
1 teaspoon oil
125 g (5 oz/¾ cup) unroasted peanuts, roughly chopped
1 teaspoon salt
½ teaspoon ground black pepper
1½ teaspoons chaat masala (page 240)

Stir together in a bowl the red onion, cucumber, tomato, coriander, chillies and lemon juice.

Heat the oil in a heavy-based frying pan over high heat, add the peanuts and salt and fry for 1 minute. Sprinkle with the pepper and the chaat masala and stir to combine. Cook for 2 minutes. Remove from the heat and add to the red onion mixture. Season with more salt just before serving. The seasoning is added at the end to prevent the ingredients from releasing too much juice before serving.

Serve in small bowls. Chucumber can be eaten with a spoon or scooped up in pieces of roti (page 178) or poppadoms.

SERVES 4

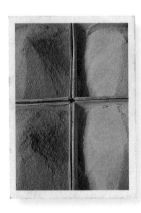 

ALOO CHAAT

Aloo chaat is a savoury snack that can be served as a potato salad or a light meal. Use salad potatoes or other waxy potatoes that hold their shape well. The tangy flavours of the chaat masala and tamarind make the salad quintessentially Indian.

1 kg (2 lb 4 oz) small salad potatoes, unpeeled
80 ml (3 fl oz/⅓ cup) tamarind purée (page 246)
4 green chillies, seeded and finely chopped

4 tablespoons chopped coriander (cilantro) leaves
2 teaspoons chaat masala (page 240)

Boil the potatoes in their skins for 15 minutes, or until just tender. Peel the potatoes and slice them into small rounds. Put them in a serving bowl.

Mix the tamarind purée with 2 tablespoons water. Add the chilli, coriander and chaat masala and mix well, then season with salt.

Gently toss the potato with the tamarind mixture and serve as a snack or as a refreshing salad on a very hot day.

SERVES 4

GOLDEN EGG CURRY

8 eggs
oil, for deep-frying
2 ripe tomatoes
25 g (1 oz) ghee
1 onion, finely chopped

1 garlic clove, finely chopped
420 ml (14 fl oz/1⅔ cups) coconut milk (page 243)
1 teaspoon ground turmeric
½ teaspoon cayenne pepper
6 curry leaves

Put the eggs in a saucepan of water and bring to the boil. Boil for 6 minutes, or until medium-hard, then cool in a bowl of cold water. Shell the eggs. You can now deep-fry the eggs if you wish. Fill a karhai or heavy-based saucepan one-third full with oil and heat it to 170°C (325°F), or until a cube of bread browns in 20 seconds when dropped in the oil. Fry the eggs in batches until golden and crisp. Drain on paper towels. Halve the eggs if you prefer.

Score a cross in the top of each tomato. Plunge into boiling water for 20 seconds, then drain and peel away from the cross. Roughly chop the flesh, discarding the cores and seeds.

Melt the ghee in a karhai or a heavy-based frying pan over low heat. Cook the onion and garlic until soft and golden. Add the chopped tomato and cook until soft. Gradually stir in the coconut milk, turmeric and cayenne, and season with salt. Bring to the boil, then reduce the heat and simmer for 2–3 minutes, until the sauce thickens slightly. Add the eggs and heat gently for 2–3 minutes. Garnish with curry leaves.

SERVES 4

STREET FOOD

*In India, there are food carts,
tea stalls and mobile snack vendors
on almost every street corner. Eating
throughout the day is a way of life
and the diversity of freshly made snacks
to choose from is incredible.*

Street food, part of the culture in India, came about after mass migration to the cities. It provides not just delicious food but a way of life, including an opportunity to socialize.

Eating street food starts as early as breakfast time when men snack on their way to work. They visit again at lunchtime when they take a break for a nourishing dish of rice and dal. In the evening, families and young couples stroll in the parks, or on the beaches, and nibble on chickpea crackers or pistachio kulfi (ice cream). At other times of the day, there is time for a refreshing glass of lassi (whipped yoghurt drink), a pani puri (deep-fried stuffed bread) or for a quick sandwich made from dubble roti (sliced bread).

Some vendors have permanent fixtures for their stalls or carts. Others (komcha-wallahs) carry baskets of foods on their heads or around their waists, or set up their karhais (cooking pots) full of bubbling oil to deep-fry little morsels, such as samosas (filled pastries), to order. The vendor with the longest queue is likely to have the best reputation and the tastiest snacks.

The food sold on the street varies regionally and is an indication of the cuisine that is popular with the locals. In the South, idlis (steamed rice cakes) and dosas (rice pancakes) feature heavily. Samosas are dunked into tamarind chutneys, and bondas (deep-fried balls of urad dal batter) are served with coconut chutney. In the North, you will find meat kebabs wrapped in roti (bread), pakoras (fritters) and bhaji (deep-fried tidbits).

Indians love to enjoy a variety of chaat when relaxing and socializing. Chaat are spicy nibbles made from a diverse range of foods ranging from fruit to puffed rice. The most famous chaat, bhel puri, appeals to all your tastebuds at once. Chaat sellers make up each type to a basic recipe, or to your specification. They add a selection of chillies for heat, tamarind chutney for sourness, plain yoghurt for cooling and chaat masala for flavour. These are spooned onto aloo ki tikki (potato cakes), stuffed into puris (puffed fried breads), sprinkled on fruit or tossed with sev (besan flour) noodle and lentils.

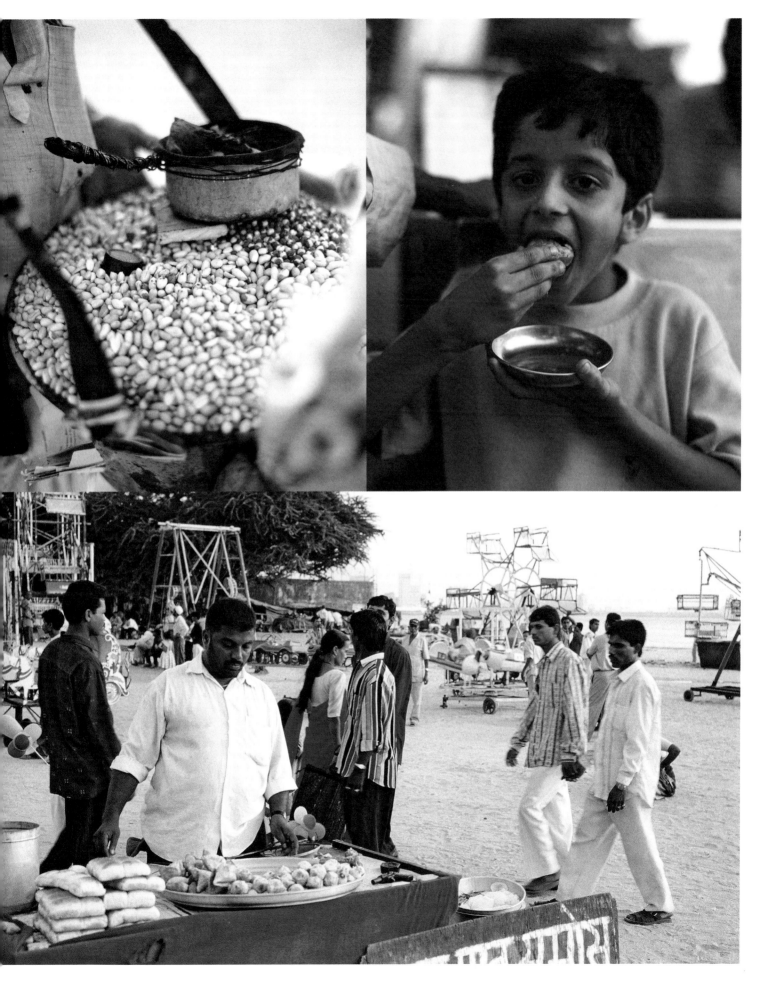

Rasam

This soup-like dish was originally known as 'mulliga thanni', literally translated as 'pepper water'. In an Indian setting, it is served spooned over rice as part of the main meal. The British version is called mulligatawny.

3 tablespoons tamarind purée (page 246)
1½ tablespoons coriander seeds
2 tablespoons cumin seeds
1 tablespoon black peppercorns
1 tablespoon oil
5 garlic cloves, skins on, roughly pounded

1 red onion, thinly sliced
2–3 dried chillies, torn into pieces
2 stalks curry leaves
200 g (7 oz) skinless, boneless chicken thighs,
　cut into small pieces

Combine the tamarind purée with 750 ml (27 fl oz/ 3 cups) water. Place a small frying pan over low heat. Dry-roast the coriander seeds until aromatic. Remove, then dry-roast the cumin seeds, followed by the black peppercorns. Grind them together using a spice grinder or a pestle and mortar.

Heat the oil in a large, heavy-based saucepan over low heat, add the garlic and onion and fry until golden. Add the chilli and the curry leaves and fry for 2 minutes, or until they are aromatic. Add the tamarind water, the ground spices and season with salt. Bring to the boil, reduce the heat and simmer for 10 minutes.

Add the chicken pieces to the pan with 250 ml (9 fl oz/1 cup) water and simmer for 20 minutes, gradually adding another 250 ml (9 fl oz/1 cup) water as the soup reduces. Remove any garlic skin that has floated to the top. Season with salt, to taste. Serve with rice (page 242).

SERVES 4

Vegetable Bhaji

These deep-fried vegetables make an excellent snack or starter. In India, street vendors line the streets all day, ducking between bicycles, cars and pedestrians while setting up stalls selling such items. Usually the busier the stall, the tastier the snack.

100 g (4 oz) carrots
100 g (4 oz) snowpeas (mangetout)
50 g (2 oz) thin eggplants (aubergines)
220 g (8 oz/2¼ cups) besan flour
1 teaspoon chilli powder
1 teaspoon ground turmeric
¼ teaspoon asafoetida
6 curry leaves
oil, for deep-frying

Cut the carrots, snowpeas and eggplants into thin sticks. Mix together the besan flour, chilli powder, turmeric, asafoetida and a pinch of salt. Pour in enough water to make a thick batter that will hold the vegetables together. Gently mix the vegetables and curry leaves into the batter.

Fill a karhai or a heavy-based saucepan one-third full with oil and heat to 180°C (350°F), or until a cube of bread browns in 15 seconds. Lower clumps of the vegetables into the oil. Fry until golden and cooked through, then drain on paper towels. Season with salt and serve hot with chutney or raita.

MAKES 20

Fry the vegetable sticks in clumps. The batter will help them stick to each other and will set around them as they cook.

Prawn Pakoras

Pakoras, known as bhajis in some places, are versatile snacks that can be made using prawns, fish pieces or vegetables. The besan flour and pomegranate seeds make a tangy flavoursome batter. Mango chutney and mint chutney go well with pakoras.

600 g (1 lb 5 oz) prawns (shrimp)
50 g (2 oz/½ cup) besan flour
1 large red onion, finely chopped
1 teaspoon dried pomegranate seeds

4 green chillies, seeded and finely chopped
2 tablespoons finely chopped coriander (cilantro) leaves
pinch of bicarbonate of soda
ghee or oil, for deep-frying

Peel and devein the prawns, then cut them into small pieces. Put the besan flour in a bowl and add 2 tablespoons of water, or enough to make a thick batter, beating with a fork to remove any lumps. Add the prawns, onion, pomegranate seeds, chilli, coriander and bicarbonate of soda, season with salt and mix well.

Fill a karhai or a heavy-based saucepan one-third full with ghee or oil and heat to 180°C (350°F), or until a cube of bread browns in 15 seconds. Drop 1 heaped teaspoon of batter at a time into the ghee or oil and deep-fry in lots of six or eight pakoras until they are brown all over. Remove and drain on paper towels. Serve hot.

MAKES 30

Deep-fry the pakoras in batches of six or eight so that the temperature of the oil remains constant. Cooking too many at once will cool the oil.

Masala Vada

100 g (4 oz) urad dal
120 g (4 oz) chana dal
2 green chillies, seeded and finely chopped
8 curry leaves, roughly chopped
½ teaspoon fennel seeds, crushed
1 red onion, finely chopped
½ teaspoon garam masala (page 240)

3 tablespoons grated coconut (page 243)
3 cm (1¼ in) piece of ginger, grated
4 tablespoons chopped coriander (cilantro) leaves
3 tablespoons rice flour or urad dal flour
pinch of baking powder (optional)
oil, for deep-frying

Soak the dal in cold water for 4 hours, then drain. Reserve 2 tablespoons of the soaked dal. Coarsely grind the remainder in a food processor or pestle and mortar. Add the reserved dal. Add the chilli, curry leaves, fennel, onion, garam masala, coconut, ginger and coriander leaves. Mix well and season with salt. Add the flour and baking powder, if using (it gives a crisper texture), then mix until the texture is soft but the dough can be shaped (you may need to add a little water). Divide the mixture into 18 portions and form each into a ball. Slightly flatten each ball to form a patty.

Fill a karhai or a heavy-based saucepan one-third full with oil and heat to 180°C (350°F), or until a cube of bread browns in 15 seconds. Fry the patties in the hot oil, in batches of four or five, until they are golden brown and crisp. Drain well on paper towels and serve hot with a chutney.

PICTURE ON PAGE 34

MAKES 18

Parsi Scrambled Eggs

2 tablespoons oil or ghee
1 red onion, finely chopped
1 garlic clove, finely chopped
2 cm (¾ in) piece of ginger, grated
1 teaspoon garam masala (page 240)
pinch of chilli powder

4 strands saffron soaked in 2 tablespoons hot milk
6 eggs
2 green chillies, finely chopped
4 slices of toast
chopped coriander (cilantro) leaves

Heat the oil or ghee in a heavy-based saucepan over low heat, add the onion and garlic and fry for 4–5 minutes, or until soft. Add the grated ginger and stir for 2 minutes, or until soft. Add the garam masala and chilli powder, along with the saffron and soaking liquid, and cook for 1 minute. Season with salt.

Whisk the eggs and add them to the saucepan. Cook over low heat, scraping the egg from the side of the pan into the centre until the mixture is soft and creamy. Remove from the heat because the eggs will continue cooking. Sprinkle the chopped chilli over the egg, then fold in. Pile onto hot toast, sprinkle with chopped coriander and serve.

SERVES 4

Masala Vada (recipe on page 33)

Kashmiri Lamb Cutlets

These cutlets are simple to make and look very good in the besan coating, which puffs around the chops and gives them a crunchy, golden crust. They are an ideal snack because the bones make them easy to pick up.

1 kg (2 lb 4 oz) lamb cutlets
3/4 teaspoon cumin seeds
1 teaspoon coriander seeds
3/4 teaspoon black peppercorns
500 ml (17 fl oz/2 cups) milk
2 cinnamon sticks
10 cardamom seeds
10 cloves

2 cm (3/4 in) piece of ginger, grated
2 onions, finely chopped
75 g (3 oz/2/3 cup) besan flour
2 teaspoons chilli powder
125 ml (4 fl oz/1/2 cup) thick plain yoghurt (page 246)
oil, for deep-frying
lime quarters

Trim the lamb of any fat and scrape the bone ends clean. Place a small frying pan over low heat and dry-roast the cumin seeds until aromatic. Remove them and dry-roast the coriander seeds. Crush the coriander and cumin seeds with the peppercorns in a spice grinder or pestle and mortar. Transfer to a large, heavy-based saucepan and add the milk, cinnamon sticks, cardamom seeds, cloves, ginger and onion. Bring to the boil over medium heat, then add the cutlets to the pan and return to the boil. Reduce the heat and simmer for 30 minutes, or until the meat is tender and very little liquid remains. Remove the cutlets and drain them.

Whisk the besan flour and chilli powder into the yoghurt with 60 ml (2 fl oz/1/4 cup) water, to make a batter.

Fill a karhai or a heavy-based saucepan one-third full of oil and heat to 180°C (350°F), or until a cube of bread browns in 15 seconds. Dip the lamb cutlets in the batter, shake off any excess, then fry them in batches in the hot oil until they are crisp. Drain on paper towels and keep them warm. Serve sprinkled with a little lime juice and salt, to taste.

SERVES 6

PORK TIKKA

Encrusted in spices and mouthwateringly tender on the inside, pork tikka is a popular dish in Punjabi dhabas (roadside restaurants) and at street stalls. It is often served with chapatis, roti or naan and chutney on the side.

MARINADE
1 onion, roughly chopped
3 garlic cloves, roughly chopped
5 cm (2 in) piece of ginger, roughly chopped
1/2 tablespoon ground cumin
1 teaspoon ground coriander
1/2 tablespoon garam masala (page 240)
1/4 teaspoon chilli powder
1/2 pinch ground black pepper
250 ml (9 fl oz/1 cup) thick plain
   yoghurt (page 246)

500 g (1 lb 2 oz) pork tenderloin, centre cut,
   cut into 2.5 cm (1 in) cubes
125 ml (4 fl oz/1/2 cup) oil
1 tablespoon garam masala (page 240)

SAUCE
1 large red onion, roughly chopped
1 garlic clove, roughly chopped
2.5 cm (1 in) piece of ginger, roughly chopped
1 green chilli, roughly chopped
25 g (1 oz/3/4 cup) coriander (cilantro) leaves

To prepare the marinade, finely chop the onion, garlic and ginger in a food processor or, if you don't have a processor, with a knife. Add the spices and yoghurt to the paste and mix through.

Put the pork in a bowl, add the marinade and mix well. Cover and marinate in the fridge for 2 hours or overnight.

To make the sauce, finely chop the onion, garlic, ginger, chilli and coriander in a food processor or, if you don't have a processor, with a knife.

Heat the oil in a large heavy-based frying pan that can fit the meat in a single layer, until sizzling but not smoking. Add the prepared sauce and stir over medium heat for 2 minutes, or until softened but not brown. Increase the heat to high and add the pork along with the marinade. Stir constantly for 5 minutes, then reduce the heat to medium and let the meat and juices bubble away for 15–20 minutes, or until the liquid has completely evaporated. The meat and dryish sauce will be a rich dark brown.

Season with salt, to taste, and sprinkle with garam masala. Cook for another 2 minutes to allow the added seasoning to be absorbed.

SERVES 4

ALOO KI TIKKI

These are potato patties sold at street food stalls in northern India. There are many variations, some of which include meat, and they are served with a variety of chutneys such as tamarind or mint and coriander. They are a good starter or snack.

500 g (1 lb 2 oz) potatoes, cut into pieces
150 g (6 oz/1 cup) fresh or frozen peas
80 ml (3 fl oz/⅓ cup) oil
2 green chillies, finely chopped
½ red onion, finely chopped
2 cm (¾ in) piece of ginger, grated

1 teaspoon ground turmeric
1 teaspoon ground cumin
1 teaspoon ground coriander
½ teaspoon garam masala (page 240)
2 tablespoons besan flour
1 tablespoon lemon juice

Cook the potatoes in boiling water for 15 minutes, or until tender enough to mash. Drain well until they are dry but still hot. Cook the peas in boiling water for 4 minutes, or until tender, then drain.

Mash the potato in a large bowl and add the peas. Heat 1 tablespoon of the oil in a small saucepan and cook the chilli, onion, ginger and spices for 1 minute, or until aromatic. Stir the mixture into the potato with the besan flour. Stir in the lemon juice and some salt. Divide into portions the size of golf balls and shape into patties.

Heat the remaining oil in a heavy-based frying pan (non-stick if you have one) and add the patties in batches. Fry them on each side until crisp and golden brown. Serve hot or cold in small dishes.

MAKES 24

Tamatar Shorba

2 tablespoons oil
1 onion, finely chopped
3 Indian bay leaves (cassia leaves)
5 cm (2 in) cinnamon stick
12 peppercorns
2 teaspoons ground cumin

2 teaspoons garam masala (page 240)
2 x 400 g (14 oz) tins chopped tomatoes
1 teaspoon sugar
250 ml (9 fl oz/1 cup) chicken stock
coriander (cilantro) leaves

Heat the oil in a heavy-based saucepan over low heat and fry the onion, bay leaves, cinnamon and peppercorns until the onion is soft. Add the cumin, garam masala and tomatoes, mashing the tomatoes with a fork to break them up. Add the sugar and stock and slowly bring to the boil. Reduce the heat and simmer over low heat for 30 minutes.

Strain the soup by pushing it through a sieve, using the back of a metal spoon to push against the solids and extract as much of the liquid as possible. Discard what's left in the sieve. Reheat, then season with salt, to taste, and garnish with the coriander leaves before serving.

SERVES 2

Tandoori Paneer

300 g (11 oz) paneer (page 245)
2 green capsicums (peppers)
1 onion
2 firm tomatoes
310 ml (11 fl oz/1¼ cups) thick plain yoghurt (page 246)
1 teaspoon ground turmeric

2 cm (¾ in) piece of ginger, grated
4 garlic cloves, crushed
1½ tablespoons lemon juice
2 tablespoons chopped mint leaves
1 tablespoon chopped coriander (cilantro) leaves
2 tablespoons oil

Cut the paneer block into 2 x 1.5 cm (¾ x ½ in) pieces. Cut the capsicums into squares, the onion into chunks and the tomatoes into cubes.

Mix the yoghurt, turmeric, grated ginger, garlic and lemon juice, together with a little salt, in a large bowl. Stir in the herbs. Add the paneer and vegetables, cover and refrigerate for 3 hours.

Preheat the grill (broiler) to its highest setting. Using eight skewers, thread onto each five pieces of paneer and some capsicum, onion and tomato. Brush with the oil, season with salt and grill (broil) on all sides for 3–4 minutes, or until the paneer and vegetables are cooked and slightly charred around the edges. Serve with roti (page 178) and a salad such as laccha (page 203).

SERVES 4

FISH AND SEAFOOD

*Seafood features prominently in many regional cuisines,
with the coast and waterways providing an abundant supply
of different varieties of fish and shellfish.*

Fish Tikka

Tikka is the Hindi word for chunk. Here, fish chunks are marinated in a blend of spices and yoghurt and cooked. In India, a tandoor, a charcoal-fired clay oven, would be used. Barbecuing is a good substitute as it also imparts a smoky flavour.

MARINADE
250 ml (9 fl oz/1 cup) thick plain yoghurt (page 246)
½ onion, finely chopped
2 cm (¾ in) piece of ginger, grated
4 garlic cloves, crushed
1 teaspoon ground coriander
2 tablespoons lemon juice
1½ tablespoons garam masala (page 240)
1 teaspoon paprika
1 teaspoon chilli powder
2 tablespoons tomato paste (concentrated purée)
1 teaspoon salt

500 g (1 lb 2 oz) skinless firm white fish such as halibut, monkfish or blue-eye
2 onions, each cut into 8 chunks
2 small green or red capsicums (peppers), each cut into 8 chunks
50 g (2 oz) cucumber, peeled and diced
1 tablespoon chopped coriander (cilantro)
250 ml (9 fl oz/1 cup) thick plain yoghurt (page 246)
lemon wedges

To make the marinade, mix the yoghurt with all the other marinade ingredients in a shallow dish that is large enough to hold the prepared skewers. You will need eight metal skewers.

Cut the fish into 24–32 bite-sized chunks. On each metal skewer, thread three or four pieces of fish and chunks of onion and capsicum, alternating as you go. Put the skewers in the marinade and turn them so that all the fish and vegetables are well coated. Cover and marinate in the refrigerator for at least 1 hour, or until you are ready to cook.

Preheat the barbecue or grill (broiler). Lift the fish skewers out of the marinade. Cook on the barbecue, or under a grill on a wire rack set above a baking tray, for 5–6 minutes, turning once, until the fish is cooked and firm and the fish and vegetables are slightly charred.

Meanwhile, stir the cucumber and coriander into the yoghurt. Serve the fish with the yoghurt and lemon wedges.

SERVES 8

SALMON CURRY

There are several stages to the making of this Goan-style dish and it takes a little time to prepare the spices and the sauce. The end result is a dry type of curry with a fairly thick sauce that works well with the rich flesh of the salmon cutlets.

SPICE MIX
6 dried chillies
1 tablespoon cumin seeds
1 teaspoon coriander seeds
1 teaspoon mustard seeds
1/4 teaspoon garam masala (page 240)
1/2 teaspoon ground turmeric

3 onions
3 tablespoons oil

1 ripe tomato, chopped
8 garlic cloves, chopped
6 green chillies, chopped
5 cm (2 in) piece of ginger, grated
125 ml (4 fl oz/1/2 cup) tamarind purée (page 246)
3 tablespoons coconut milk powder or coconut cream (page 243)
1 kg (2 lb 4 oz) salmon cutlets

Prepare the spice mix by grinding the chillies with the cumin, coriander and mustard seeds to a fine powder using a spice grinder or pestle and mortar, then mixing with the garam masala and turmeric.

Thinly slice one of the onions, and finely chop the other two onions. Heat the oil over low heat in a heavy-based frying pan large enough to hold the pieces of fish in a single layer. Add the sliced onion and fry until golden. Add the tomato, remaining onion, garlic, chilli and ginger and cook, stirring occasionally, for 20 minutes, or until the oil has separated from the sauce.

Add the spice mix and the tamarind purée to the pan and bring to the boil. Add the coconut milk powder or coconut cream and stir until well mixed. Season with salt, to taste. Add the fish and bring slowly to the boil. The sauce is not very liquid but it needs to be made very hot in order to cook the fish. Simmer for 5 minutes, then turn the fish over and simmer for another 5 minutes, or until the fish is cooked through and the sauce is thick.

SERVES 6

Rohu Kalia

4–6 tablespoons mustard oil
850 g (1 lb 14 oz) skinless rohu, salmon, halibut
   or cod fillets, cut into large chunks
5 cm (2 in) cinnamon stick
5 cardamom pods
4 cloves
4 Indian bay leaves (cassia leaves)
1 onion, finely chopped

4 garlic cloves, crushed
7 cm (2¾ in) piece of ginger, grated
½ teaspoon ground turmeric
1 teaspoon ground cumin
1 teaspoon chilli powder (optional)
500 ml (17 fl oz/2 cups) thick plain yoghurt (page 246)
3 green chillies, shredded

Heat the oil in a karhai or heavy-based frying pan over medium heat and fry the fish a few pieces at a time until golden brown. Drain on paper towels. Add more oil, if necessary, and fry the cinnamon, cardamom, cloves and bay leaves over low heat for 1 minute. Add the onion and fry for 5 minutes, or until golden. Add the garlic, ginger, turmeric, cumin and chilli powder, if using, and fry for 30 seconds.

Remove from the heat and stir in the yoghurt, a little at a time, to prevent it from curdling. Return the pan to low heat, add the green chilli and bring to the boil. Season with salt. Slide in the fish and return to the boil. Reduce the heat and simmer for 10 minutes, or until the fish flakes easily and is cooked through. Serve immediately.

SERVES 4

Prawns with Green Mango

250 g (9 oz) tiger prawns (shrimp)
1½ teaspoons chilli powder
1 teaspoon ground turmeric
½ teaspoon yellow mustard seeds
½ teaspoon cumin seeds
4 garlic cloves, roughly chopped

4 cm (1½ in) piece of ginger, roughly chopped
1 red onion, roughly chopped
80 ml (3 fl oz/⅓ cup) oil
1 red onion, thinly sliced
1 green unripe mango, finely chopped

Peel and devein the tiger prawns, leaving their tails intact.

Put the chilli powder, turmeric, mustard seeds, cumin seeds, garlic, ginger and chopped red onion in a blender, food processor or pestle and mortar and process to form a paste. If necessary, add a little water.

Heat the oil in a karhai or heavy-based frying pan and fry the sliced onion. When it starts to brown, add the curry paste and fry until aromatic. Add the prawns and 185 ml (6 fl oz/¾ cup) water, cover and simmer for 3–4 minutes, or until the prawns are cooked through and they start to curl up. Add the green mango and cook for another 1–2 minutes to thicken the curry. Season with salt.

SERVES 4

Fish with Kokum

3 x 5 cm (2 in) pieces kokum or 2 tablespoons tamarind
    purée (page 246)
4 ripe tomatoes
2 tablespoons oil
1 teaspoon black mustard seeds
½ teaspoon fenugreek seeds
3 cm (1¼ in) piece of ginger, grated
4 green chillies, slit in half

1 garlic clove, crushed
2 onions, sliced
1 teaspoon ground turmeric
1 tablespoon ground coriander
250 ml (9 fl oz/1 cup) coconut milk (page 243)
800 g (1 lb 12 oz) skinless pomfret, sole or leatherjacket
    fillets, cut into large chunks
1 stalk of curry leaves

Rinse the kokum pieces, remove any stones and put the kokum in a bowl with cold water for a few minutes to soften. Drain the kokum and slice it into pieces.

Meanwhile, score a cross in the top of each tomato. Plunge them into boiling water for 20 seconds, then drain and peel away from the cross. Roughly chop the tomatoes, discarding the cores and seeds and reserving any juices.

Heat the oil in a karhai or deep, heavy-based frying pan over low heat and cook the mustard seeds until they start to pop. Add the fenugreek, ginger, chilli, garlic and onion and cook until the onion is soft. Fry the turmeric and coriander for 2 minutes. Add the coconut milk, tomato and kokum. Bring to the boil. Reduce the heat and simmer for 5 minutes. Add the fish and simmer for 2–3 minutes, or until the fish flakes easily and is cooked through. Season with salt and add the curry leaves.

SERVES 6

Food Journey

SEAFOOD

India has about 7000 kilometres of coastline split between its east and west coasts. It also has a large network of backwaters, rivers, tanks (reservoirs) and ponds, all of which teem with fish and crustaceans.

Fish dishes abound in the cuisines of Bengal, Maharashtra, Kerala and Goa. And, although seawater fish are popular in Maharashtra, Goa and Kerala on the western coast, freshwater fish are more highly prized in Bengal in the east. Everything caught is utilized.

Tiny fish are eaten whole and large fish such as shark, swordfish or king mackerel are cut into fillets or cutlets. Prawns (shrimp), both seawater and freshwater, are used all over India. Crabs and lobsters are eaten on the coast or in restaurants. Bivalves, including oysters, clams (vongole) and mussels, are eaten on the west coast. In the areas where fresh fish are not available, dried fish such as the renowned Bombay duck are used.

Fishing itself takes place in many forms. Most fish are caught from small boats, or by individual fishermen, rather than from large commercial vessels. The Koli fishermen in Mumbai (Bombay) are known for their deep-sea fishing. They put out to sea in colourful fishing boats. In Kerala, fish are caught in Chinese fishing nets or from snake boats rowed out to sea. There are also individuals with rods and nets stationed by virtually every pond, river and tank at some stage during the day, catching fish for that day's meals.

Fish is bought from wet fish stalls at markets, or direct from the dock or beach. In Kochi (Cochin) in Kerala, fish is sold by a fast-talking auctioneer from a large rectangle of blue plastic mat laid out on the shore or beach. Each batch of fish or prawns (shrimp) is tipped onto the plastic and haggled over before being scooped up and then spirited away to be cleaned and cooked. At the Sassoon Docks in Mumbai (Bombay), huge quantities of seafood are unloaded onto the quay, then sold out of baskets. The scene is a colourful melee of women, fishermen, commercial buyers and private shoppers.

Fish caught locally are not only eaten in India but are also sold, fresh and frozen, to the international market. Prized fish particular to Indian cuisine, such as hilsa, rohu and pomfret, are airfreighted to be sold to Indian communities worldwide. Other seafood such as tuna and prawns (shrimp), suitable for the markets in Japan and Europe, are flown there daily.

FISH IN BANANA LEAF

This traditional way of preparing fish in Bengal often uses hilsa (elish), a favourite fish of the area. Mustard oil is an important ingredient in Bengali cooking and gives a unique flavour to dishes, though if unavailable you can use sunflower oil instead.

4 x 120 g (4 oz) pieces hilsa (elish) or blue-eye fillet, skinned
1½ tablespoons lemon juice
½ teaspoon salt
3 tablespoons brown mustard seeds
5 cm (2 in) piece of ginger, chopped

4 green chillies, chopped
3 teaspoons mustard oil
¼ teaspoon ground turmeric
1 teaspoon chilli powder
4 pieces young banana leaf, or foil, cut into neat pieces big enough to wrap the fish

Wash the fish and pat dry with paper towels. Mix the lemon juice and salt and rub into the fish.

Grind the mustard seeds to a powder in a spice grinder or a pestle and mortar. Put the mustard, ginger, green chilli, mustard oil, turmeric and chilli powder in a food processor or a pestle and mortar and grind to a smooth paste. Dip the banana leaves in very hot water to soften them. Wipe dry as the pieces become pliant.

Smear the fish with the paste to thoroughly coat. Grease the leaves, or foil, with oil. Place a piece of fish and some marinade in the centre of each and loosely fold into a parcel. Tie with kitchen string and put in a steamer over a saucepan of simmering water. Cover and steam for 10–12 minutes. Open a parcel to check that the fish flakes easily and is cooked. Serve in the banana leaves.

SERVES 4

PRAWN CURRY WITH TAMARIND

500 g (1 lb 2 oz) tiger prawns (shrimp)
1/2 teaspoon fennel seeds
1 tablespoon oil
2 cinnamon sticks
3 cardamom pods
1 large onion, finely chopped

5 garlic cloves, crushed
2 cm (3/4 in) piece of ginger, grated
1 stalk of curry leaves
1 teaspoon ground turmeric
1 teaspoon chilli powder
1 1/2 tablespoons tamarind purée (page 246)

Peel and devein the prawns, leaving the tails intact. Place a small frying pan over low heat and dry-fry the fennel seeds until aromatic.

Heat the oil in a karhai or heavy-based frying pan and fry the fennel seeds, cinnamon, cardamom and onion until the onion is brown.

Stir in the garlic, ginger and curry leaves, then add the prawns, turmeric, chilli powder and tamarind. Toss over high heat until the prawn tails turn pink and the prawns are cooked through. Remove from the heat and season with salt, to taste.

SERVES 4

CURRIED SQUID

1 kg (2 lb 4 oz) fresh squid
1 teaspoon cumin seeds
1 teaspoon coriander seeds
1 teaspoon chilli powder
1/2 teaspoon ground turmeric
2 tablespoons oil
1 onion, finely chopped

10 curry leaves
1/2 teaspoon fenugreek seeds
4 garlic cloves, crushed
7 cm (2 3/4 in) piece of ginger, grated
4 tablespoons coconut milk powder mixed with
   170 ml (6 fl oz/2/3 cup) water
3 tablespoons lime juice

Pull the squid heads and tentacles out of the bodies, along with any innards, and discard. Peel off the skins. Rinse the bodies, pulling out the clear quills, then cut the bodies into 2.5 cm (1 in) rings.

Place a small frying pan over low heat and dry-fry the cumin seeds until aromatic. Remove, then dry-fry the coriander seeds. Grind both to a fine powder with the chilli and turmeric, using a spice grinder or pestle and mortar. Mix the spices with the squid.

Heat the oil in a karhai or heavy-based frying pan and fry the onion until lightly browned. Add the curry leaves, fenugreek, garlic, ginger and coconut milk. Bring slowly to the boil. Add the squid, then stir well. Simmer for 2–3 minutes, or until cooked and tender. Stir in the lime juice, season and serve.

SERVES 4

CREAMY PRAWN CURRY

This coconut-flavoured prawn curry is a speciality of Bengal. Traditionally, the prawns are cooked inside a partially matured coconut. Care should be taken not to overcook the prawns or they will become rubbery.

500 g (1 lb 2 oz) tiger prawns (shrimp)
1½ tablespoons lemon juice
3 tablespoons oil
½ onion, finely chopped
½ teaspoon ground turmeric
5 cm (2 in) cinnamon stick
4 cloves
7 cardamom pods

5 Indian bay leaves (cassia leaves)
2 cm (¾ in) piece of ginger, grated
3 garlic cloves, chopped
1 teaspoon chilli powder
50 g (2 oz) creamed coconut mixed with 170 ml
    (6 fl oz/⅔ cup) water, or 170 ml (6 fl oz/⅔ cup)
    coconut milk (page 243)

Peel and devein the prawns, leaving the tails intact. Put them in a bowl, add the lemon juice, then toss together and leave them for 5 minutes. Rinse the prawns under cold running water and pat dry with paper towels.

Heat the oil in a karhai or heavy-based frying pan and fry the onion until lightly browned. Add the turmeric, cinnamon, cloves, cardamom, bay leaves, ginger and garlic, and fry for 1 minute. Add the chilli powder, creamed coconut or coconut milk, and salt, to taste, and slowly bring to the boil. Reduce the heat and simmer for 2 minutes.

Add the prawns, return to the boil, then reduce the heat and simmer for 5 minutes, or until the prawns are cooked through and the sauce is thick.

PICTURE ON PAGE 60

SERVES 4

Creamy Prawn Curry (recipe on page 59)

Molee

A molee is a rich creamy dish popular in Kerala on India's west coast where it is made with local fish. There are many versions, some very hot. This one is fairly mild and therefore perfect for those who don't like fiery food. You can adapt it to your taste.

1 tablespoon oil
1 large onion, thinly sliced
3 garlic cloves, crushed
2 small green chillies, finely chopped
2 teaspoons ground turmeric
1 teaspoon ground coriander
1 teaspoon ground cumin

4 cloves
6 curry leaves, plus extra, to serve
420 ml (14 fl oz/1²/₃ cups) coconut milk (page 243)
½ teaspoon salt
600 g (1 lb 5 oz) pomfret, sole or leatherjacket fillets, skinned
1 tablespoon chopped coriander (cilantro) leaves

Heat the oil in a karhai or a deep, heavy-based frying pan, add the onion and cook for 5 minutes. Add the garlic and chilli and cook for another 5 minutes, or until the onion has softened and looks translucent. Add the turmeric, coriander, cumin and cloves and stir-fry with the onion for 2 minutes. Stir in the curry leaves, coconut milk and salt and bring to just below boiling point. Reduce the heat and simmer for 20 minutes.

Cut each fish fillet into two or three large pieces and add them to the sauce. Return the sauce to simmering point and cook for 5 minutes, or until the fish is cooked through and flakes easily. Check the seasoning, add more salt if necessary, then stir in the coriander leaves. Garnish with curry leaves.

SERVES 6

CHILLI CRAB

This recipe combines sweet-tasting crab meat with aromatic spices and the heat from chillies. Provide your guests with a crab cracker, picks, finger bowls and pieces of roti to mop up the wonderful juices. You can use any kind of crab for this recipe.

4 x 250 g (9 oz) small live crabs or 2 x 500 g (1 lb 2 oz)
   live crabs
125 ml (4 fl oz/½ cup) oil
2 garlic cloves, crushed
4 cm (1½ in) piece of ginger, grated
½ teaspoon ground cumin
½ teaspoon ground coriander

¼ teaspoon ground turmeric
¼ teaspoon cayenne pepper
1 tablespoon tamarind purée (page 246)
1 teaspoon sugar
2 small red chillies, finely chopped
2 tablespoons chopped coriander (cilantro) leaves

Put the whole crabs in the freezer for 2 hours to immobilize them. Using a large, heavy-bladed knife or cleaver, cut off the large front claws from each crab, then twist off the remaining claws. Turn over each body and pull off each apron piece, then pull out and discard the spongy grey gills. Cut each crab in half (quarters if you are using large crabs). Crack the large front claws with the handle of a cleaver or a rolling pin. Rinse off any chips of shell and pat dry with paper towels.

Mix half the oil with the garlic, ginger, cumin, coriander, turmeric, cayenne pepper, tamarind, sugar, chilli and a generous pinch of salt until they form a paste. Heat the remaining oil in a karhai or large, heavy-based, deep frying pan over medium heat. Add the spice paste and stir for 30 seconds, or until aromatic.

Add the crab portions to the frying pan and cook, stirring for 2 minutes, making sure the spice mix gets rubbed into the cut edges of the crab. Add 60 ml (2 fl oz/¼ cup) of water, cover and steam the crabs, tossing a couple of times during cooking, for another 5–6 minutes, or until cooked through. The crabs will turn pink or red when they are ready and the flesh will go opaque (make sure the large front claws are well cooked). Drizzle a little of the liquid from the pan over the crabs, scatter with coriander leaves and serve.

SERVES 4

Far left: To prepare the crabs, first pull off the large front claws and set them aside.

Left: Pull open the body and remove the spongy grey gills.

Chapter 3

POULTRY AND MEAT

Butter chicken, rogan josh, lamb madras, pork vindaloo and tandoori chicken ... considering so many Indians follow a vegetarian diet, there is a remarkable array of meat recipes.

ആരോഗ്യത്തിനും കൂടുതൽ പാലിനും

കേ.വ്
കാലിത
MITED, IRINJALAK

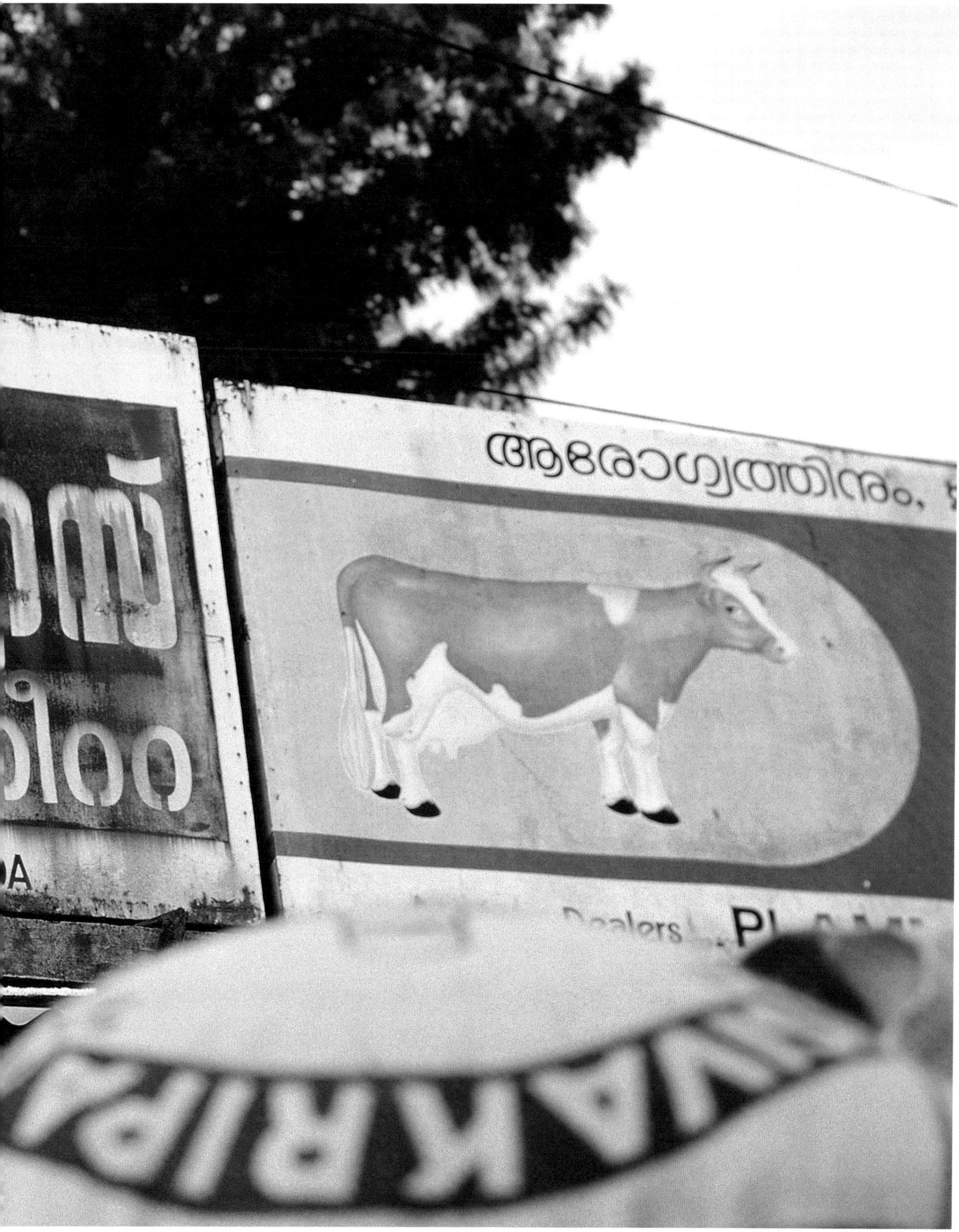
ആരോഗ്യത്തിനും.
Dealers

PARSI CHICKEN WITH APRICOTS

In this delicious Parsi dish from Mumbai (Bombay), the use of dried apricots, jaggery and vinegar gives a sweet–sour flavour. The potato straws make an unusual garnish and add a contrasting crunchy texture to enhance the recipe.

1.5 kg (3 lb 5 oz) chicken or chicken pieces
3 tablespoons oil
2 large onions, thinly sliced
1 clove garlic, finely chopped
4 cm (1½ in) piece of ginger, finely chopped
3 dried chillies
1½ teaspoons garam masala (page 240)
2 tablespoons tomato paste (concentrated purée)
1 teaspoon salt

2 tablespoons clear vinegar
1½ tablespoons jaggery or soft brown sugar
12 dried apricots

POTATO STRAWS
1 large waxy potato, coarsely grated
1 tablespoon salt
oil, for deep-frying

If using a whole chicken, cut it into eight pieces by removing the legs and cutting between the thigh and drumstick joint. Cut along either side of the backbone and remove it. Turn the chicken over and cut through the cartilage down the centre of the breastbone. Cut each breast in half, leaving the wing attached. Trim off the wing tips.

Heat the oil in a karhai or flameproof casserole over medium heat. Cook the onion until soft and starting to brown. Stir in the garlic, ginger, chillies and garam masala, then add the chicken. Stir and brown the chicken for 5 minutes, taking care not to burn the onion. Add the tomato paste, salt and 250 ml (9 fl oz/1 cup) water. Bring to the boil,

then reduce the heat, cover and simmer gently for 20 minutes. Add the vinegar, jaggery and apricots, cover and simmer for 15 minutes.

To make the potato straws, combine the potato, salt and 1.5 litres (52 fl oz/6 cups) water in a large bowl. Squeeze the potato a handful at a time, then pat dry on a tea towel (dish towel). Fill a karhai or deep, heavy-based saucepan one-third full with oil and heat to 160°C (315°F), or until a cube of bread browns in 30 seconds. Add a small handful of the potato. Cook until golden and crisp, then drain on paper towels. Cook all the potato in the same way.

Serve the chicken topped with the potato straws.

SERVES 4

Rogan Josh

There are many curry pastes available for making this classic dish. However, nothing compares with a version made with freshly ground spices. The colour comes from the chilli powder and paprika. In Kashmir, red cockscomb flowers are used for colour.

8 garlic cloves, crushed
6 cm (2½ in) piece of ginger, grated
2 teaspoons ground cumin
1 teaspoon Kashmiri chilli powder
2 teaspoons paprika
2 teaspoons ground coriander
1 kg (2 lb 4 oz) boneless leg or shoulder of lamb,
    cut into 3 cm (1¼ in) cubes
5 tablespoons ghee or oil

1 onion, finely chopped
6 cardamom pods
4 cloves
2 Indian bay leaves (cassia leaves)
8 cm (3 in) cinnamon stick
185 ml (6 fl oz/¾ cup) thick plain yoghurt (page 246)
4 strands saffron, mixed with 2 tablespoons milk
¼ teaspoon garam masala (page 240)

Mix the garlic, ginger, cumin, chilli, paprika and coriander in a large bowl. Add the meat and stir thoroughly to coat well. Cover and marinate for at least 2 hours, or overnight, in the refrigerator.

Heat the ghee or oil in a karhai or flameproof casserole over low heat. Add the onion and cook for 10 minutes, or until lightly browned. Remove from the pan.

Add the cardamom pods, cloves, bay leaves and cinnamon to the pan and fry for 1 minute. Increase the heat to high, add the meat and onion, then mix well and cook for 2 minutes. Stir well, then reduce the heat to low, cover and cook for 15 minutes.

Uncover and fry for 3 minutes, or until the meat is quite dry. Add 125 ml (4 fl oz/½ cup) water, cover and cook for 5–7 minutes, or until the water has evaporated and the oil has separated. Fry the meat for another 1–2 minutes, then add 250 ml (9 fl oz/ 1 cup) water. Cover and cook for 40–50 minutes, gently simmering until the meat is tender and the liquid is reduced.

Stir in the yoghurt when the meat is almost tender, taking care not to allow the meat to catch on the base of the pan. Add the saffron with the milk. Stir the mixture a few times to mix in the saffron. Season with salt, to taste. Remove from the heat and sprinkle with the garam masala.

SERVES 6

Spicy Roast Chicken in Banana Leaves

In this recipe, the chicken is wrapped in banana leaves before it is roasted. This creates a distinctive aroma and flavour. Enclosing it in banana leaves also keeps the chicken moist and succulent while it cooks. For a special occasion, serve it with plain pulao.

2 kg (4 lb 8 oz) chicken
3 tablespoons lemon juice
1 teaspoon salt
1 tablespoon oil
2 large onions, roughly chopped
4 garlic cloves, crushed
4 cm (1½ in) piece of ginger, roughly chopped

3 tablespoons ground almonds
½ teaspoon chilli powder
1 teaspoon ground turmeric
2 teaspoons garam masala (page 240)
3 coriander (cilantro) roots, chopped
4 tablespoons chopped coriander (cilantro) leaves
3–4 young banana leaves

Trim off any excess fat from the chicken. Pat the chicken completely dry with paper towels and prick all over with a skewer so the marinade can penetrate the flesh. Rub the lemon juice and salt over the skin and inside the cavity of the chicken.

Heat the oil in a heavy-based frying pan over low heat and cook the onion until it starts to brown. Add the garlic and ginger and cook for 2 minutes, or until soft. Add the almonds, chilli, turmeric and garam masala and cook for 1 minute. Allow the onion mixture to cool completely.

Place the cooled mixture in a food processor or a pestle and mortar, along with the coriander roots and leaves. Grind to a smooth paste and rub the paste thoroughly all over the chicken and inside the cavity. Cover and refrigerate the chicken for at least 6 hours or overnight.

Preheat the oven to 200°C (400°F/Gas 6). Dip the banana leaves into very hot water to soften them. Wipe the leaves dry as they become pliant.

Tie the legs of the chicken together to keep them in place. Wrap the chicken in the banana leaves, making sure that it is well covered. Tie a piece of kitchen string around the chicken like a parcel. If you can't buy banana leaves, wrap the chicken in a large sheet of foil. Place the chicken in a roasting tin and bake for 1½ hours. Unwrap the banana leaves or foil from around the top of the chicken, baste with some of the juices and return it to the oven for 10 minutes, or until well browned. Check that the chicken is cooked by pulling away one of the legs – the juices should run clear. Rest the chicken for 10 minutes before carving.

SERVES 6

LAMB MADRAS

Traditionally in India, hogget (sheep) or goat meat is often the only meat available. As goat can be tough when cooked this way, we have used lamb. It is cooked slowly so the sauces are absorbed and the curry matures to a full flavour.

1 kg (2 lb 4 oz) boneless leg or shoulder of lamb, cut into 2.5 cm (1 in) cubes
1½ teaspoons ground turmeric
2 tablespoons coriander seeds
2 teaspoons cumin seeds
10 dried chillies
12 curry leaves, plus extra, to serve
10 garlic cloves, roughly chopped
5 cm (2 in) piece of ginger, roughly chopped
1 teaspoon fennel seeds
1 tablespoon tamarind purée (page 246)
4 tablespoons oil or ghee
3 large onions, sliced
625 ml (22 fl oz/2½ cups) coconut milk (page 243)
8 cm (3 in) cinnamon stick
6 cardamom pods

Rub the cubed lamb with the ground turmeric. Place a small frying pan over low heat and dry-roast the coriander seeds until aromatic. Remove and dry-roast the cumin seeds, then repeat with the chillies. Grind them all to a powder in a pestle and mortar or spice grinder. Add six curry leaves, the garlic and ginger and grind to a paste.

Dry-roast the fennel seeds in the pan until they brown and start to pop. Dissolve the tamarind in 125 ml (4 fl oz/½ cup) hot water.

Heat the oil or ghee in a karhai or flameproof casserole over low heat and cook the onion for 5–10 minutes, or until soft. Add the chilli paste and cook for a few minutes until aromatic. Add the meat and toss well to mix with the paste.

Add 500 ml (17 fl oz/2 cups) of the coconut milk and 60 ml (2 fl oz/¼ cup) water. Bring to the boil, then reduce the heat to medium and simmer for 10 minutes, or until the liquid has reduced.

Add the remaining coconut milk, the cinnamon stick, cardamom pods and fennel seeds. Season with salt and pepper. Cover and cook, partially covered over medium heat, for 1 hour, or until the meat is tender, stirring occasionally. Add the tamarind purée and check the seasoning. Stir until the oil separates out from the meat, then spoon it off or blot with paper towels before removing the pan from the heat.

Stir well and add the remaining six curry leaves. Garnish with more curry leaves.

SERVES 6

Saag Gosht

This is a richly flavoured, traditional dish from the northern part of India. It is cooked until the sauce is very thick. It can be served with either rice or breads. If you can't buy fresh spinach, you can use defrosted, drained, frozen spinach instead.

2 teaspoons coriander seeds

1½ teaspoons cumin seeds

oil, for cooking

1 kg (2 lb 4 oz) boneless leg or shoulder of lamb,
    cut into 2.5 cm (1 in) cubes

4 onions, finely chopped

6 cloves

6 cardamom pods

10 cm (4 in) cinnamon stick

10 black peppercorns

4 Indian bay leaves (cassia leaves)

3 teaspoons garam masala (page 240)

¼ teaspoon ground turmeric

1 teaspoon paprika

8 cm (3 in) piece of ginger, grated

4 garlic cloves, crushed

185 ml (6 fl oz/¾ cup) thick plain yoghurt (page 246)

450 g (1 lb) English spinach or amaranth leaves,
    roughly chopped

Place a small frying pan over low heat and dry-roast the coriander seeds until aromatic. Remove them and dry-roast the cumin seeds. Grind the seeds to a fine powder using a spice grinder or pestle and mortar.

Heat 3 tablespoons of the oil in a karhai or a flameproof casserole over low heat. Brown a few pieces of meat at a time. Remove from the pan. Add a little more oil to the pan and fry the onion, cloves, cardamom, cinnamon stick, peppercorns and bay leaves until the onion is lightly browned. Add the cumin and coriander, garam masala, turmeric and paprika and fry for 30 seconds.

Add the meat, ginger, garlic, yoghurt and 420 ml (14 fl oz/1⅔ cups) water and bring to the boil. Reduce the heat to a simmer, cover and cook for 1½–2 hours, or until the meat is very tender and most of the water has evaporated. If it hasn't, remove the lid, increase the heat and fry until the moisture has evaporated. Season with salt, to taste.

Cook the spinach briefly in simmering water until it is just wilted, then refresh in cold water. Drain thoroughly, then finely chop. Squeeze out any extra water by squeezing the spinach between two plates. Add to the lamb and cook for 3 minutes, or until well combined and any extra liquid has evaporated.

SERVES 6

Kashmiri Chicken

This chicken dish, combining nuts and saffron, is delicately flavoured with a creamy sauce. To make the spices more aromatic, it is best to dry-roast them as suggested in the recipe, rather than use ready-ground ones.

1.5 kg (3 lb 5 oz) chicken or chicken pieces
6 cardamom pods
1/2 teaspoon coriander seeds
1/2 teaspoon cumin seeds
2 cm (3/4 in) cinnamon stick
8 peppercorns
6 cloves
100 g (4 oz/2/3 cup) blanched almonds

75 g (3 oz/1/2 cup) shelled pistachios
2 tablespoons ghee or oil
1 onion, finely chopped
4 garlic cloves, finely chopped
5 cm (2 in) piece of ginger, finely chopped
125 ml (4 fl oz/1/2 cup) chicken stock
250 ml (9 fl oz/1 cup) thick plain yoghurt (page 246)
1/2 teaspoon saffron threads

If using a whole chicken, cut it into eight pieces by removing the legs and cutting between the thigh and drumstick joint. Cut along either side of the backbone and remove it. Turn the chicken over and cut through the cartilage down the centre of the breastbone. Remove the skin from the chicken and cut the flesh off the bones and then into bite-sized pieces. (Reserve the carcass for making stock if you wish.)

Remove the seeds from the cardamom pods. Place a small frying pan over low heat and dry-roast the coriander seeds until aromatic. Remove and dry-roast the cumin seeds, then the piece of cinnamon stick. Grind the cardamom seeds, roasted spices, peppercorns and cloves to a fine powder using a

spice grinder or pestle and mortar. Finely chop the almonds and pistachios in a food processor or in a spice grinder, or with a knife.

Heat the ghee or oil in a karhai or a flameproof casserole over low heat and cook the onion until golden brown. Add the garlic, ginger and chicken pieces and fry rapidly for about 5 minutes. Add the ground spices and the chicken stock and then simmer, covered tightly for 30 minutes.

Stir the ground almonds and pistachios into the yoghurt. Mix the saffron with 1 teaspoon of hot water. Add the yoghurt and the saffron to the pan and bring to the boil. Reduce the heat and simmer, uncovered, for 10 minutes. Season with salt.

SERVES 4

Moghul-style Lamb

For this dish, the lamb is marinated before it is cooked. This ensures that the meat is tender and full of flavour. The cream is added to temper the strong combination of the spices.

6 garlic cloves, roughly chopped
4 cm (1½ in) piece of ginger, roughly chopped
50 g (2 oz/⅓ cup) blanched almonds
2 onions, thinly sliced
750 g (1 lb 10 oz) boneless leg or shoulder of lamb, cut into 2.5 cm (1 in) cubes
2 teaspoons coriander seeds
40 g (1½ oz) ghee

7 cardamom pods
5 cloves
1 cinnamon stick
1 teaspoon salt
310 ml (11 fl oz/1¼ cups) cream
½ teaspoon cayenne pepper
½ teaspoon garam masala (page 240)
flaked toasted almonds

Blend the garlic, ginger, almonds and 50 g (2 oz) of the onion in a blender or food processor. If you don't have a blender, finely chop them with a knife or grind together in a pestle and mortar. Add a little water if necessary to make a smooth paste, then put in a bowl with the lamb cubes and mix thoroughly to coat the meat. Cover and marinate in the refrigerator for 2 hours, or overnight.

Place a small frying pan over low heat and dry-roast the coriander seeds until aromatic, then grind them to a fine powder using a spice grinder or a pestle and mortar.

Heat the ghee in a karhai or flameproof casserole. Add the cardamom pods, cloves and cinnamon stick and, after a few seconds, add the remaining onion and fry until it is soft and starting to brown. Transfer the onion to a plate.

Fry the meat and the marinade in the pan until the mixture is quite dry and has started to brown a little. Add 170 ml (6 fl oz/⅔ cup) hot water to the pan, cover tightly and cook over low heat for 30 minutes, stirring occasionally.

Add the ground coriander, salt, cream, cayenne pepper and cooked onion to the pan, cover and simmer, stirring occasionally, for 30 minutes, or until the lamb is tender. Remove the cardamom pods, cloves and cinnamon stick, then stir in the garam masala. Sprinkle with flaked almonds.

SERVES 4

Chicken Tikka

MARINADE
2 teaspoons paprika
1 teaspoon chilli powder
2 tablespoons garam masala (page 240)
1/4 teaspoon tandoori food colouring
1 1/2 tablespoons lemon juice
4 garlic cloves, roughly chopped

5 cm (2 in) piece of ginger, roughly chopped
15 g (1/2 oz/1/2 cup) coriander (cilantro) leaves, chopped
125 ml (4 fl oz/1/2 cup) thick plain yoghurt (page 246)

500 g (1 lb 2 oz) skinless chicken breast fillets,
    cut into cubes
wedges of lemon

For the marinade, blend the ingredients in a food processor until smooth, or chop the garlic, ginger and coriander leaves more finely and mix with the rest of the marinade ingredients. Season with salt.

Put the chicken cubes in a bowl with the marinade and mix thoroughly. Cover and marinate overnight in the refrigerator.

Preheat the oven to 200°C (400°F/Gas 6). Thread the chicken onto four metal skewers and put them on a metal rack above a baking tray. Roast for 15–20 minutes, or until the chicken is cooked through and browned around the edges. Serve with wedges of lemon to squeeze over the chicken.

SERVES 4

Chicken Tikka Masala

1 tablespoon oil
1 onion, finely chopped
2 cardamom pods
2 garlic cloves, crushed
400 g (14 oz) tin chopped tomatoes
1/4 teaspoon ground cinnamon
1 tablespoon garam masala (page 240)

1/2 teaspoon chilli powder
1 teaspoon jaggery or soft brown sugar
310 ml (11 fl oz/1 1/4 cups) cream
1 tablespoon ground almonds
1 quantity chicken tikka (above)
1 tablespoon chopped coriander (cilantro) leaves

Heat the oil in a karhai or a heavy-based saucepan over low heat. Add the onion and cardamom pods and cook until the onion is soft and just starting to brown. Add the garlic to the pan and cook for 1 minute, then add the tomato and cook until the paste is thick.

Add the cinnamon, garam masala, chilli and sugar to the pan and cook for 1 minute. Stir in the cream and almonds, then add the cooked chicken tikka pieces and gently simmer for 5 minutes, or until the chicken is heated through. Garnish with the chopped coriander.

SERVES 6

Fried Beef Kerala

oil, for deep-frying, plus 2 tablespoons oil
1 potato, cut into small cubes
500 g (1 lb 2 oz) rump steak, thinly sliced
3 garlic cloves, crushed
1 teaspoon ground black pepper
1 tablespoon ginger juice (page 246)
2 onions, sliced in rings

60 ml (2 fl oz/¼ cup) beef stock
2 tablespoons tomato paste (concentrated purée)
2 teaspoons soy sauce
1 teaspoon chilli powder
60 ml (2 fl oz/¼ cup) lemon juice
3 tomatoes, chopped
80 g (3 oz/½ cup) fresh or frozen peas

Fill a deep, heavy-based saucepan one-third full with oil and heat it to 180°C (350°F), or until a cube of bread browns in 15 seconds. Deep-fry the potato until golden brown. Drain on paper towels.

Put the steak in a bowl and toss with the garlic, pepper and ginger juice. Heat the extra oil and fry the beef quickly in batches over high heat. Keep each batch warm as you remove it. Reduce the heat and fry the onion until golden, then remove.

Cook the beef stock, tomato paste, soy sauce, chilli and lemon juice in the pan over medium heat until reduced. Add the onion, cook for 3 minutes, stir in the tomato and peas, then cook for 1 minute. Add the beef and potato and toss until heated through.

PICTURE ON PAGE 86

SERVES 4

Goan Beef Curry

8 cardamom pods
10 cm (4 in) cinnamon stick
8 cloves
3 teaspoons coriander seeds
3 teaspoons cumin seeds
1 teaspoon fennel seeds
½ teaspoon fenugreek seeds
½ teaspoon ground black pepper
125 ml (4 fl oz/½ cup) oil

2 onions, finely chopped
6 garlic cloves, finely chopped
10 cm (4 in) piece of ginger, grated
1 kg (2 lb 4 oz) braising or stewing steak, cut into cubes
½ teaspoon ground turmeric
2 teaspoons chilli powder
100 g (4 oz) creamed coconut, dissolved in 310 ml
   (11 fl oz/1¼ cups) water, or 310 ml (11 fl oz/1¼ cups)
   coconut milk (page 243)

Remove the seeds from the cardamom pods and grind to a fine powder in a spice grinder or pestle and mortar with the cinnamon, cloves, coriander, cumin, fennel, fenugreek and black pepper.

Heat the oil in a karhai or heavy-based frying pan over medium heat and fry the onion, garlic and ginger until lightly browned. Add the meat and fry until browned. Add the spices and fry for 1 minute. Add the creamed coconut and bring slowly to the boil. Cover, reduce the heat and simmer for 1 hour, or until the meat is tender. If the liquid evaporates, add 185 ml (6 fl oz/¾ cup) boiling water and stir to make a thick sauce. Season with salt.

SERVES 6

Fried Beef Kerala (recipe on page 85)

METHI GOSHT

In India, methi is the name for fenugreek. In northern India, methi leaves are often combined with lamb (gosht) and served as a delicacy. Methi produces a distinctive aromatic flavour in this dish. Serve with Indian breads or rice.

2 onions, roughly chopped
4 garlic cloves, roughly chopped
8 cm (3 in) piece of ginger, roughly chopped
3 green chillies (seed them for less heat)
125 ml (4 fl oz/½ cup) oil
2 Indian bay leaves (cassia leaves)
1 kg (2 lb 4 oz) boneless lamb leg or shoulder, cut into 2.5 cm (1 in) cubes

1 tablespoon ground cumin
2 tablespoons ground coriander
½ teaspoon garam masala (page 240)
½ teaspoon chilli powder
2 teaspoons salt
½ teaspoon ground black pepper
4 bunches of fresh methi leaves, finely chopped (about 200 g/7 oz)

Blend the onion, garlic, ginger and chillies in a blender or food processor until finely chopped. If you don't have a blender, finely chop them together with a knife or crush them in a pestle and mortar.

Heat the oil in a karhai or a large flameproof casserole over medium heat and add the chopped mixture and the bay leaves. Cook for 3 minutes, or until golden and just starting to catch on the base of the pan. Add the lamb in batches, stirring for about 20 minutes, until it is all browned. The juices of the meat will start to run clear and the oil will separate out. You need to keep stirring or the meat will catch on the base of the pan.

Add all the spices, and the salt and pepper, and fry for 3 minutes, or until all pieces of the lamb are thoroughly coated. Add 185 ml (6 fl oz/¾ cup) water and bring to the boil, then reduce the heat, cover and simmer for 45 minutes, adding a little more water if necessary. The sauce should be dryish rather than sloppy. Gently stir in the methi leaves and cook for another 15 minutes, or until the oil separates from the lamb and the sauce has turned a rich olive green.

SERVES 4

Lamb Korma

This mild dish, which comes in many guises, needs to be cooked very slowly to let the subtle flavours emerge. This version uses white poppy seeds and cashew nuts to thicken the sauce and yoghurt to make it creamy.

1 kg (2 lb 4 oz) boneless leg or shoulder of lamb,
    cut into 2.5 cm (1 in) cubes
2 tablespoons thick plain yoghurt (page 246)
1 tablespoon coriander seeds
2 teaspoons cumin seeds
5 cardamom pods
2 onions
2 tablespoons grated coconut (page 243)

1 tablespoon white poppy seeds (khus khus)
3 green chillies, roughly chopped
4 garlic cloves, crushed
5 cm (2 in) piece of ginger, grated
25 g (1 oz) cashew nuts
6 cloves
1/4 teaspoon ground cinnamon
2 tablespoons oil

Put the meat in a bowl, add the yoghurt and mix to coat thoroughly.

Place a small frying pan over low heat and dry-roast the coriander seeds until aromatic. Remove, and then dry-roast the cumin seeds. Grind the roasted mixture to a fine powder using a spice grinder or pestle and mortar. Remove the seeds from the cardamom pods and grind them.

Roughly chop one onion and thinly slice the other. Put the roughly chopped onion with the ground spices, coconut, poppy seeds, chilli, garlic, ginger, cashew nuts, cloves and cinnamon in a blender, add 170 ml (6 fl oz/2/3 cup) of water and process to a smooth paste. If you don't have a blender, crush

everything together in a pestle and mortar, or finely chop with a knife, before adding the water.

Heat the oil in a karhai or a flameproof casserole over medium heat. Add the remaining onion and fry until lightly browned. Pour the blended spice mixture into the pan, season with salt and cook over low heat for 1 minute, or until the liquid has evaporated and the sauce has thickened.

Add the lamb with the yoghurt and slowly bring to the boil. Cover tightly and simmer, stirring occasionally, for about 1 1/2 hours, or until the meat is very tender. If the water has evaporated during this time, add 125 ml (4 fl oz/1/2 cup) of water to make a sauce. The sauce should be quite thick.

SERVES 4

Dhansak

A flavoursome Parsi dish that is served at special occasions, this version has evolved from a lavish recipe that used even more types of dal. The combination of different types of dal gives a varied texture but you can use just masoor or toor.

100 g (4 oz) toor dal (yellow lentils)
25 g (1 oz) moong dal
25 g (1 oz) chickpeas
50 g (2 oz) masoor dal (red lentils)
1 eggplant (aubergine), unpeeled
150 g (6 oz) pumpkin, unpeeled
150 g (6 oz) amaranth or English spinach leaves
2 tomatoes
2 green chillies
2 tablespoons ghee or oil
1 onion, finely chopped

3 garlic cloves, crushed
2 cm (3/4 in) piece of ginger, grated
1 kg (2 lb 4 oz) boneless leg or shoulder of lamb, cut into 3 cm (1¼ in) cubes
2 cm (3/4 in) cinnamon stick
5 cardamom pods, bruised
3 cloves
1 tablespoon ground coriander
1 teaspoon ground turmeric
1 teaspoon chilli powder, or to taste
3 tablespoons lime juice

Soak the toor dal, moong dal and chickpeas in plenty of water for about 2 hours. Drain well.

Put all four types of pulse in a saucepan, add 1 litre (35 fl oz/4 cups) of water, cover and bring to the boil. Reduce the heat and simmer, uncovered, for 15 minutes, skimming off any scum that forms on the surface, and stirring occasionally to make sure all the pulses are cooking at the same rate and are soft. Lightly mash the pulses to a similar texture.

Cook the eggplant and pumpkin in boiling water for 10–15 minutes, or until soft. Scoop out the pumpkin flesh and cut it into pieces. Carefully peel the eggplant (it may be very pulpy) and cut it into pieces. Cut the amaranth or spinach into 5 cm (2 in) lengths. Halve the tomatoes and split the chillies lengthwise, removing any seeds.

Heat the ghee or oil in a karhai or flameproof casserole and fry the onion, garlic and ginger for 5 minutes, or until lightly brown and softened. Add the lamb and brown for about 10 minutes, or until aromatic. Add the cinnamon, cardamom pods, cloves, ground coriander, ground turmeric and chilli powder and cook for 5 minutes to allow the flavours to develop. Add 170 ml (6 fl oz/⅔ cup) water, cover and simmer for 40 minutes, or until the lamb is tender.

Add the mashed lentils and all the cooked and raw vegetables to the pan. Season with the lime juice and salt and pepper. Simmer for 15 minutes (if the sauce is too thick, add a little water). Stir well, then check the seasoning. The dhansak should be flavoursome, aromatic, tart and spicy.

SERVES 6

Mangalorean Pork Bafath

Mangalorean food is south Indian with many other influences, including Portuguese. This recipe is mildly sweet because of the Kashmiri chillies. The pork has oils that almost roast the spices within the meat giving a beautiful, aromatic result.

20 red Kashmiri chillies, seeded
2 teaspoons coriander seeds
1 teaspoon cumin seeds
½ teaspoon ground turmeric
10 black peppercorns
2 tablespoons tamarind purée (page 246)
1.5 kg (3 lb 5 oz) boneless pork leg or shoulder, cut into 3 cm (1¼ in) cubes
1 tablespoon oil

2 onions, cut into 3 cm (1¼ in) pieces
2 cm (¾ in) piece of ginger, finely chopped
6 green chillies, slit lengthwise into halves
8 cloves
2 cm (¾ in) cinnamon stick, pounded roughly
1 tablespoon dark vinegar
3 garlic cloves, finely chopped
1 green chilli, extra, seeded, finely sliced lengthwise

Place a small frying pan over low heat and dry-fry the chillies, coriander seeds, cumin seeds, ground turmeric and peppercorns until aromatic. Grind the mixture to a fine powder using a spice grinder or pestle and mortar. Mix with the tamarind purée and meat. Cover and marinate in the refrigerator for 2 hours.

Heat the oil in a karhai or a flameproof casserole over high heat, add the meat mixture in batches and brown all over. Return all the meat to the pan, then add the onion, ginger, chilli, cloves and cinnamon. Stir thoroughly to mix with the pork.

Reduce the heat to low and cook for 20 minutes, or until the meat juices appear and mix with the spice, creating a thick sauce.

Add the vinegar, garlic and 250 ml (9 fl oz/1 cup) water and cook for 1–1¼ hours, until the pork is very tender. Season with salt, to taste. Cook until the oil separates from the spice mixture, which indicates the meat is ready. You can skim off the oil or blot it from the surface with paper towels if you prefer. Garnish with the chilli before serving.

SERVES 6

Far left: Removing the seeds from the chillies will make the dish slightly milder.

Left: Gently stir the spices to evenly roast them.

Memsahib's Lamb Raan

This dish looks impressive even though it can be made without much fuss. It is excellent for dinner or a special lunch, but it does need to be marinated overnight so the flavours can permeate the lamb. Serve it with a couple of vegetable dishes and some rice.

1.7 kg (3 lb 12 oz) leg of lamb
coriander (cilantro) leaves (optional)

MARINADE
1 teaspoon cardamom seeds
1 onion, roughly chopped
4 garlic cloves, roughly chopped
2 cm (3/4 in) piece of ginger, roughly chopped
3 green chillies, seeded
2 teaspoons ground cumin

1/2 teaspoon ground cloves
1 1/2 tablespoons lemon juice
250 ml (9 fl oz/1 cup) thick plain yoghurt (page 246)

ALMOND COATING
3 tablespoons blanched almonds
1 tablespoon jaggery or soft brown sugar
125 ml (4 fl oz/1/2 cup) thick plain yoghurt (page 246)
1/2 teaspoon red food colouring (optional)

Trim the excess fat from the lamb and stab the meat all over with a skewer so that the marinade will penetrate.

To make the marinade, grind the cardamom seeds to a fine powder using a spice grinder or pestle and mortar. Chop the onion, garlic, ginger and chillies to a paste using a blender or food processor. If you don't have a processor, finely chop them with a knife, then grind to a paste in a pestle and mortar. Mix in the ground cardamom seeds, the cumin and cloves. Add the lemon juice and yoghurt and mix well.

Using half the marinade, thickly coat the lamb all over. Cover with plastic wrap and marinate in the refrigerator overnight. Cover the remaining marinade and refrigerate until needed.

To make the almond coating, preheat the oven to 190°C (375°F/Gas 5). Finely chop the almonds in a food processor or with a knife. Mix the reserved marinade with the ground almonds, sugar, yoghurt and food colouring, if using. Coat the lamb all over with the mixture, especially on the top and sides. Transfer the lamb to a shallow roasting tin and cover loosely with oiled foil. Bake for 1 hour, then remove the foil and bake for another 30 minutes, or until the lamb is cooked and the coating is set and browned. Test the meat nearest to the bone to see whether it is cooked – a skewer should come out very hot. Carefully press on any of the almond coating that has dropped off during cooking.

Carve the meat at the table for full effect. Garnish with coriander, if using. Top each serving with a little of the almond coating.

SERVES 6

Food Journey

SPICES

✧◦✧◦✧◦✧◦✧◦✧◦✧◦✧◦✧◦✧◦✧◦✧◦✧◦✧◦✧◦✧◦✧◦✧

Spices became important items of commerce early in the evolution of trade. They were small, easily transported and often worth their weight in gold.

India was essentially 'discovered' by Vasco da Gama in May 1498 as he searched for the 'Indies', the origin of the spices that were arriving in Europe via Arab traders. It is said that he came ashore and shouted "for Christ and for spices". The discovery of the spice coast of India had a profound effect on the European spice trade as it broke the stranglehold of the Arabs and cut out the middlemen.

Cloves and nutmeg were taken by Muslim traders from Malacca to southern India where black pepper and cinnamon (from Kerala and Sri Lanka) were added to the cargo. The whole lot was then sold on to Europe from the spice ports on the west coast of India. The use of maritime trading routes meant that war, religious differences and other disruptions to the overland routes did not upset the flow of spices to Europe. This kept their prices relatively constant and affordable. The next logical step was to grow spices, like cloves and nutmeg, in southern India that had only previously been available from the Moluccas.

Kochi (Cochin) in Kerala became a bustling spice port in 1341 after a flood in the area created a natural harbour. The area around Mattancherry is still busy with major trading and carts of spices trundle back and forth between the wholesale dealers and their godowns (warehouses) all day.

Amongst the spices of India, pepper, cardamom, nutmeg, mace, ginger, vanilla and turmeric are all grown in Kerala and Tamil Nadu, seed spices such as coriander, cumin, dill and fennel are found in Gujarat and Rajasthan, and chillies grow in every state and union territory in India. Precious saffron is cultivated in Kashmir, fenugreek in Uttar Pradesh and mustard in Andhra Pradesh.

Spices have a strong association with Indian food of all types and Indian cuisine is probably the most highly spiced in the world. In the North, spices are often dry-roasted and ground before use, warming mixtures such as garam masala are used and chillies are not always important. In the South, spices are ground with coconut or fresh herbs to make a wet paste, and a seasoning (tarka) of mustard seeds, curry leaves and dried chilli, all fried in oil, may be stirred into the dish at the end of cooking.

BUTTER CHICKEN

Butter chicken, or murgh makhni, is a Moghul dish that has many versions. The butter in the title refers to ghee, a type of clarified butter. Rice is an ideal accompaniment and pieces of roti or naan can be used to mop up the delicious juices.

2 cm (³/₄ in) piece of ginger, roughly chopped
3 garlic cloves, roughly chopped
80 g (3 oz/½ cup) blanched almonds
170 ml (6 fl oz/²/₃ cup) thick plain yoghurt (page 246)
½ teaspoon chilli powder
¼ teaspoon ground cloves
¼ teaspoon ground cinnamon
1 teaspoon garam masala (page 240)
4 cardamom pods, lightly crushed

400 g (14 oz) tin chopped tomatoes
1¼ teaspoons salt
1 kg (2 lb 4 oz) skinless, boneless chicken thighs,
    cut into fairly large pieces
5 tablespoons ghee or clarified butter
1 large onion, thinly sliced
6 tablespoons finely chopped coriander (cilantro) leaves
4 tablespoons thick (double/heavy) cream

Blend the ginger and garlic together to a paste in a food processor or pestle and mortar, or crush the garlic and finely grate the ginger and mix together. Grind the almonds in a food processor or finely chop with a knife. Put the paste and almonds in a bowl with the yoghurt, chilli, cloves, cinnamon, garam masala, cardamom pods, tomato and salt, and blend together with a fork. Add the chicken pieces and stir to coat thoroughly. Cover and marinate for 2 hours, or overnight, in the fridge.

Preheat the oven to 180°C (350°F/Gas 4). Heat the ghee or clarified butter in a karhai or a deep, heavy-based frying pan, add the onion and fry until softened and browned.

Add the chicken mixture and fry for 2 minutes. Mix in the fresh coriander. Put the mixture into a shallow baking dish, pour in the cream and stir with a fork.

Bake for 1 hour. If the top is browning too quickly during cooking, cover with a piece of foil. Leave to rest for 10 minutes before serving. The oil will rise to the surface. Just before serving, place the dish under a hot grill (broiler) for about 2 minutes to brown the top. Before serving, tip the dish and spoon off any extra oil.

SERVES 6

KOFTA IN TOMATO AND YOGHURT SAUCE

Every nation seems to have a version of kofta, ranging from meatballs and croquettes to rissoles and dumplings. This recipe is the north Indian way of preparing them. The rich tomato and yoghurt sauce is perfect when served with naan bread.

KOFTA
1 onion
500 g (1 lb 2 oz) minced (ground) lamb
2 cm (3/4 in) piece of ginger, grated
3 garlic cloves, finely chopped
2 green chillies, seeded and finely chopped
1/2 teaspoon salt
1 egg

TOMATO AND YOGHURT SAUCE
2 teaspoons coriander seeds
2 teaspoons cumin seeds
3 tablespoons oil

10 cm (4 in) cinnamon stick
6 cloves
6 cardamom pods
1 onion, finely chopped
1/2 teaspoon ground turmeric
1 teaspoon paprika
1 teaspoon garam masala (page 240)
1/2 teaspoon salt
200 g (7 oz) tin chopped tomatoes
170 ml (6 fl oz/2/3 cup) thick plain yoghurt (page 246)

coriander (cilantro) leaves

To make the kofta, grate the onion, put it in a sieve and use a spoon to press out as much of the liquid as possible. Put the onion in a bowl with the lamb, ginger, garlic, chilli, salt and egg. Mix thoroughly, then divide into 20 portions and shape each into a ball. Cover with plastic wrap and refrigerate for 2 hours. Alternatively, the meatballs can be put in the freezer while the sauce is being prepared, then they will be firm enough to hold their shape when added to the sauce.

To make the sauce, place a small frying pan over low heat and dry-roast the coriander seeds until aromatic. Remove, then dry-roast the cumin seeds. Grind the roasted mixture to a fine powder using a spice grinder or pestle and mortar.

Heat the oil in a karhai or a heavy-based frying pan over low heat. Add the cinnamon stick, cloves, cardamom pods and onion and fry until the onion is golden. Add all the ground spices and salt and fry for 30 seconds. Stir in the tomato, then remove from the heat and slowly stir in the yoghurt.

Return the pan to the heat, slide in the meatballs and bring to the boil. Simmer over very low heat, uncovered, for 1 hour. It may be necessary to shake the pan from time to time to prevent the meatballs from sticking. If the sauce dries out during cooking, add 125 ml (4 fl oz/1/2 cup) water as required and continue to cook for the full hour. Remove any whole spices before serving and serve garnished with coriander leaves.

SERVES 4

TANDOORI CHICKEN

Traditionally cooked in a tandoor (clay oven), this is perhaps the most popular chicken dish from northern India, where it is served with naan and laccha. You can never get exactly the same results at home but this is a very good approximation.

1.5 kg (3 lb 5 oz) chicken or skinless chicken thighs
   and drumsticks
2 tablespoons ghee
onion rings, to serve
lemon wedges, to serve

MARINADE
2 teaspoons coriander seeds
1 teaspoon cumin seeds
1 onion, roughly chopped

3 garlic cloves, roughly chopped
5 cm (2 in) piece of ginger, roughly chopped
250 ml (9 fl oz/1 cup) thick plain yoghurt (page 246)
grated rind of 1 lemon
3 tablespoons lemon juice
2 tablespoons clear vinegar
1 teaspoon paprika
2 teaspoons garam masala (page 240)
1/2 teaspoon tandoori food colouring (optional)

If using a whole chicken, remove the skin and cut the chicken in half. Using a sharp knife, make 2.5 cm (1 in) long diagonal incisions on each limb and breast, taking care not to cut through to the bone. If using thighs and drumsticks, trim away any excess fat and make an incision in each piece.

For the marinade, heat a frying pan over low heat and dry-roast the coriander seeds until aromatic. Remove and dry-roast the cumin seeds. Grind the roasted seeds to a fine powder using a spice grinder or pestle and mortar. In a food processor, blend all the marinade ingredients to form a smooth paste. Season with salt. If you don't have a food processor, chop the onion, garlic and ginger more finely and mix with the rest of the ingredients in a bowl.

Add the chicken to the spicy yoghurt marinade and refrigerate for at least 8 hours, or overnight. Turn the chicken occasionally in the marinade to ensure that all sides are soaked.

Preheat the oven to 200°C (400°F/Gas 6). Place the chicken on a wire rack on a baking tray. Cover with foil and roast on the top shelf for 45–50 minutes, or until cooked through (test by inserting a skewer into a thigh – the juices should run clear). Baste the chicken with the marinade once during cooking. Remove the foil 15 minutes before the end of cooking, to brown the tandoori mixture. Preheat the grill (broiler) to its highest setting.

Prior to serving, while the chicken is still on the rack, heat the ghee, pour it over the chicken halves and cook under the grill (broiler) for 5 minutes to blacken the edges of the chicken like a tandoor.

Serve the chicken garnished with the onion rings and lemon wedges. The chicken pieces can also be grilled (broiled), barbecued or spit-roasted.

SERVES 4

Murgh Masala

This is a mild dish that originated in northern India. Because of its subtle flavour, it is suitable for serving at any meal. A combination of tomatoes, ginger and spices gives flavouring, and the yoghurt enriches the sauce.

1.5 kg (3 lb 5 oz) skinless chicken thighs
  or chicken pieces
2 teaspoons ground cumin
2 teaspoons ground coriander
1½ teaspoons garam masala (page 240)
¼ teaspoon ground turmeric
2 onions, finely chopped
4 garlic cloves, roughly chopped

5 cm (2 in) piece of ginger, roughly chopped
2 very ripe tomatoes, chopped
3 tablespoons oil or ghee
5 cloves
8 cardamom pods
5 cm (2 in) cinnamon stick
10 curry leaves
170 ml (6 fl oz/⅔ cup) thick plain yoghurt (page 246)

Trim off any excess fat or skin from the chicken. Mix the cumin, coriander, garam masala and turmeric together and rub it into the chicken.

Put half the onion, the garlic, ginger and chopped tomato in a food processor and blend to a smooth paste. If you don't have a blender, finely chop the ingredients and mix them together.

Heat the oil or ghee in a karhai or flameproof casserole over low heat, add the remaining onion, the cloves, cardamom, cinnamon and curry leaves and fry until the onion is golden brown. Add the tomato and onion paste and stir for 5 minutes. Season with salt, to taste. Add the spiced chicken, stir in the yoghurt and bring slowly to the boil.

Reduce the heat, cover and simmer for 50 minutes, or until the oil has separated from the sauce. Stir the ingredients occasionally to prevent the chicken from sticking. If the sauce is too thin, simmer for a couple of minutes with the lid off. Season with salt, to taste.

SERVES 4

Kheema Matar

During the winter months, when peas are in season in northern India, this dry-style lamb curry is often served with ubiquitous vegetable dishes such as aloo gobi and aloo methi. Leave out the chillies for a mild version.

2 onions, roughly chopped
4 garlic cloves, roughly chopped
5 cm (2 in) piece of ginger, roughly chopped
4 green chillies
170 ml (6 fl oz/²/₃ cup) oil
2 Indian bay leaves (cassia leaves)
500 g (1 lb 2 oz) minced (ground) lamb
pinch of asafoetida
2 tablespoons tomato paste (concentrated purée)
¼ teaspoon ground turmeric

½ teaspoon chilli powder
2 tablespoons ground coriander
2 tablespoons ground cumin
2 tablespoons thick plain yoghurt (page 246)
3 teaspoons salt
1 teaspoon ground black pepper
235 g (9 oz/1½ cups) fresh or frozen peas
¼ teaspoon garam masala (page 240)
5 tablespoons finely chopped coriander (cilantro)

Put the onion, garlic, ginger and two of the chillies in a food processor and process until very finely chopped. If you don't have a food processor, finely chop the ingredients or grind them together in a pestle and mortar.

Heat the oil in a karhai or heavy-based frying pan over medium heat. Add the onion mixture and the bay leaves and fry for 3–4 minutes, or until golden brown. Add the lamb and cook for 15 minutes, stirring occasionally to prevent the meat sticking. Break up any lumps of meat with the back of a fork. Add the asafoetida and tomato paste, stir and reduce the heat to a simmer.

Add the turmeric, chilli powder, ground coriander and ground cumin and stir for 1 minute. Add the yoghurt, salt and pepper and continue frying for 5 minutes. Add 185 ml (6 fl oz/³/₄ cup) water, a little at a time, stirring after each addition until it is well absorbed. Add the peas and the remaining whole chillies, stir well, then cover and simmer for 20 minutes, or until the peas are cooked through. (If using frozen peas, cook the lamb and chillies for 15 minutes, then add the peas and cook for 5 minutes.) Add the garam masala and chopped coriander and stir for 1 minute before serving.

PICTURE ON PAGE 110   SERVES 4

Kheema Matar (recipe on page 109)

Pork Vindaloo

Vindaloo is notorious for being hot and spicy, and was invented by the Portuguese in Goa. The name is Portuguese for 'vinegar and garlic'. The vinegar is made from coconut (clear) and molasses (dark) but white and balsamic can be used instead.

1 kg (2 lb 4 oz) leg of pork on the bone
6 cardamom pods
4 dried chillies
10 cm (4 in) cinnamon stick, roughly broken
1 teaspoon black peppercorns
1 teaspoon cloves
1 teaspoon cumin seeds
1/2 teaspoon coriander seeds
1/2 teaspoon ground turmeric
1/4 teaspoon fenugreek seeds

80 ml (3 fl oz/1/3 cup) clear vinegar
1 tablespoon dark vinegar
80 ml (3 fl oz/1/3 cup) oil
2 onions, thinly sliced
10 garlic cloves, thinly sliced
5 cm (2 in) piece of ginger, cut into matchsticks
3 ripe tomatoes, roughly chopped
4 green chillies, chopped
1 teaspoon jaggery or soft brown sugar

Trim any excess fat from the pork, remove the bone and cut the pork into 2.5 cm (1 in) cubes. Reserve the bone.

Split open the cardamom pods and remove the seeds. Finely grind the cardamom seeds, dried chillies, cinnamon, peppercorns, cloves, cumin seeds, coriander seeds, turmeric and fenugreek seeds in a spice grinder or pestle and mortar.

In a large bowl, mix the ground spices together with the vinegars. Add the pork and mix to coat well. Cover and marinate in the refrigerator for 3 hours.

Heat the oil in a karhai or flameproof casserole over low heat. Fry the onion until lightly browned. Add the garlic, ginger, tomato and chilli and stir well. Add the pork, increase the heat to high and fry for 3–5 minutes, or until browned. Add 250 ml (9 fl oz/1 cup) water and any marinade liquid left in the bowl, reduce the heat and bring slowly back to the boil. Add the jaggery and the pork bone. Cover tightly and simmer for 1 1/2 hours, stirring occasionally until the meat is very tender. Discard the bone. Season with salt, to taste.

SERVES 4

VEGETABLES

Indian cuisine utilizes a wide selection of vegetables prepared with fresh herbs and aromatic spices to produce tantalizing vegetable dishes.

METHI ALOO

The scented aroma and distinctive flavour of methi (fresh fenugreek) transforms any dish. Methi aloo can be served with most Indian main meals. Methi can be bought from shops that specialize in Indian foods.

1 small onion, roughly chopped
2 garlic cloves, roughly chopped
2.5 cm (1 in) piece of ginger, roughly chopped
80 ml (3 fl oz/⅓ cup) oil
¼ teaspoon ground turmeric
600 g (1 lb 5 oz) potatoes, cut into cubes
2 green chillies, seeded and finely chopped
¼ teaspoon chilli powder

½ teaspoon ground cumin
½ teaspoon ground coriander
3 teaspoons salt
½ teaspoon ground black pepper
2 bunches of methi (about 140 g/5 oz of methi leaves), roughly chopped
unsalted butter (optional)

Put the onion, garlic and ginger in a food processor and chop together, but not to a paste, or chop with a knife and mix together.

Heat the oil in a karhai or heavy-based frying pan over medium heat and fry the onion mixture until softened. Stir in the turmeric. Add the potato and chilli and fry for 5 minutes. Add the chilli, cumin, coriander, salt and pepper and stir for 1 minute.

Add 2 tablespoons water to the pan, cover, reduce the heat and simmer. As the potato cooks, it might start sticking to the pan, so after 10 minutes, add 2 more tablespoons of water if necessary. At no stage should the potato be allowed to brown.

After 10 minutes, stir in the methi and cook over low heat for 15 minutes, or until the potato is soft. Season with salt, to taste. Serve with a knob of unsalted butter melted on top if you like.

SERVES 4

SPICY EGGPLANT

This is a wonderful dish in which eggplant pieces are cooked with pickling-style spices. It can be served as part of an Indian feast or as a spicy accompaniment. The eggplant is also good as a vegetarian main dish with rice and some yoghurt.

800 g (1 lb 12 oz) eggplants (aubergines), cut into wedges 5 cm (2 in) long
400 g (14 oz) ripe tomatoes or 400 g (14 oz) tin chopped tomatoes
2.5 cm (1 in) piece of ginger, grated
6 garlic cloves, crushed
310 ml (11 fl oz/1¼ cups) oil

1 teaspoon fennel seeds
½ teaspoon kalonji (nigella seeds)
1 tablespoon ground coriander
¼ teaspoon ground turmeric
½ teaspoon cayenne pepper
1 teaspoon salt

Put the eggplant pieces in a colander, sprinkle with salt and leave them for 30 minutes to allow any of the bitter juices to run out. Rinse, squeeze out any excess water, then pat dry with paper towels.

If using fresh tomatoes, score a cross in the top of each and plunge into boiling water for 20 seconds. Drain and peel away from the cross. Roughly chop the tomatoes, discarding the cores and seeds and reserving any juices.

Purée the ginger and garlic with one-third of the tomato in a blender or food processor. If you don't have a blender, finely chop the tomatoes and mix with the ginger and garlic.

Heat 125 ml (4 fl oz/½ cup) of the oil in a large, deep, heavy-based frying pan and when hot, add as many eggplant pieces as you can fit in a single layer. Cook over medium heat until brown on both sides, then transfer to a sieve over a bowl to drain off the excess oil. Add the remaining oil as needed and cook the rest of the eggplant in batches.

Reheat the oil left in the pan and add the fennel seeds and kalonji. Cover and allow to pop for a few seconds. Add the tomato and ginger mixture and the remaining ingredients, except the eggplant. Cook, stirring regularly for 5–6 minutes, until the mixture is thick and fairly smooth (be careful as it may spit). Carefully add the eggplant so the pieces stay whole, cover and cook gently for 10 minutes.

Store the eggplant in the sauce in the fridge. Pour off any excess oil before serving. The eggplant can either be served cold or gently warmed through.

SERVES 6

Gajar Matar

In northern India, peas (matar) from Simla, in Himachal Pradesh, are famous for their sweet flavour. They are often served with carrots in winter when both vegetables are in season. Gajar matar is a staple vegetable dish that goes well with all Indian meals.

1 small onion, roughly chopped
1 garlic clove, roughly chopped
2.5 cm (1 in) piece of ginger, chopped
125 ml (4 fl oz/½ cup) oil
1 teaspoon cumin seeds
1½ teaspoons ground turmeric
325 g (11 oz) carrots, diced
1 teaspoon ground cumin

1 teaspoon ground coriander
250 g (9 oz/1⅔ cups) peas
3 teaspoons salt
¼ teaspoon sugar
¼ teaspoon chilli powder
4 teaspoons pomegranate seeds (optional)
½ teaspoon garam masala (page 240)

Put the onion, garlic and ginger in a food processor and blend until finely chopped, or chop them with a knife and mix together.

Heat the oil in a karhai or frying pan over high heat and cook the onion mixture for 2 minutes, or until softened. Reduce the heat and add the cumin seeds and turmeric. When the seeds are sizzling, add the carrot and stir for 2 minutes. Add the ground cumin and coriander and fry for 2 minutes. Stir in the peas, salt, sugar and chilli. Add 2 tablespoons water if using frozen peas, or 4 tablespoons if using fresh. Reduce the heat to a simmer, add the pomegranate seeds, if using, and stir before partially covering the pan. Simmer for 15 minutes, or until the carrot and peas are tender. Stir in the garam masala.

SERVES 6

Cabbage with Split Peas

125 g (5 oz) split peas
450 g (1 lb) green cabbage, shredded
3 tablespoons oil
¼ teaspoon black mustard seeds
2 teaspoons cumin seeds

8 curry leaves
2 dried chillies
pinch of asafoetida
¼ teaspoon ground turmeric
coriander (cilantro) leaves (optional)

Soak the split peas in 750 ml (27 fl oz/3 cups) of boiling water for 2 hours. Drain thoroughly.

Shred the cabbage. Heat the oil in a karhai or a deep, heavy-based frying pan over low heat. Add the mustard and cumin seeds, cover and allow to pop briefly. Add the curry leaves, dried chillies and split peas and fry for 5 minutes, stirring often. Add the asafoetida, turmeric and cabbage and cook over low heat until the cabbage is cooked through and tender. Season with salt, to taste. Serve garnished with coriander leaves if you wish.

SERVES 4

Saag Paneer

Leafy greens are used in many recipes from the north to the south of India. In this recipe, spinach, tomatoes and paneer are used in a more textured dish than the smooth puréed versions served in many northern Indian restaurants.

1 bunch (500 g/1 lb 2 oz) English spinach leaves
½ teaspoon ground cumin
½ teaspoon ground coriander
½ teaspoon fenugreek seeds
1 tablespoon oil
1 red onion, thinly sliced

5 garlic cloves, chopped
200 g (7 oz) tin chopped tomatoes
2 cm (¾ in) piece of ginger, grated
1 teaspoon garam masala (page 240)
225 g (8 oz) or ½ quantity paneer (page 245), cubed

Blanch the spinach in boiling water for 2 minutes. Refresh in cold water, drain and very finely chop.

Place a small frying pan over low heat. Dry-roast the ground cumin until aromatic. Remove and set aside, then dry-roast the ground coriander, then the fenugreek seeds.

Heat the oil in a karhai or heavy-based frying pan over low heat and fry the onion, garlic, and roasted spices until brown and aromatic. Stir in the tomato, ginger and garam masala. Bring to the boil. Add the spinach and cook until the liquid has reduced. Fold in the paneer, trying to keep it whole. Stir gently until heated through. Season with salt.

SERVES 4

Shebu Bhaji

Dill is a herb that can be used in abundance, as it is in this dish, without being overpowering. It has a mild but very distinctive flavour. Indian dill is similar to European dill and they are interchangeable in this recipe.

200 g (7 oz) potatoes
200 g (7 oz) dill
2 tablespoons oil
2 garlic cloves, chopped

1 dried chilli
¼ teaspoon ground turmeric
1 teaspoon black mustard seeds
pinch of asafoetida

Cut the potatoes into 2.5 cm (1 in) cubes. Cook in a saucepan of simmering water for 15 minutes, or until just tender. Drain well.

Wash the dill in several changes of water and trim off the tough stalks. Roughly chop the dill.

Heat the oil in a heavy-based saucepan and fry the garlic over low heat for 30 seconds. Add the chilli, turmeric, mustard seeds and asafoetida, cover and briefly allow the seeds to pop. Stir in the potatoes until well mixed. Add the dill, cover and cook over low heat for 5 minutes. Season with salt.

SERVES 2

Cauliflower with Mustard

This is a lovely dish using cauliflower and many spices. In India, the variations of this dish all put the emphasis on quite different spice combinations. This one goes well with rice and pieces of roti but is also a good accompaniment to meat dishes.

2 teaspoons yellow mustard seeds
2 teaspoons black mustard seeds
1 teaspoon ground turmeric
1 teaspoon tamarind purée (page 246)
2–3 tablespoons mustard oil or oil

2 garlic cloves, finely chopped
½ onion, finely chopped
600 g (1 lb 5 oz) cauliflower, broken into small florets
3 mild green chillies, seeded and finely chopped
2 teaspoons kalonji (nigella seeds)

Grind the mustard seeds together to a fine powder in a spice grinder or pestle and mortar. Mix with the turmeric, tamarind purée and 125 ml (4 fl oz/ ½ cup) water to form a smooth, liquid paste.

Heat 2 tablespoons oil in a karhai or large, heavy-based saucepan over medium heat. Reduce the heat to low, add the garlic and onion and fry until golden. Cook the cauliflower in batches, adding more oil if necessary, and fry until lightly browned. Add the chilli and fry for 1 minute, or until tinged with brown around the edges.

Return all the cauliflower to the pan, sprinkle it with the mustard mixture and kalonji and stir well. Increase the heat to medium and bring to the boil, even though there is not much sauce. Reduce the heat to low, cover and cook until the cauliflower is nearly tender and the seasoning is dry. You may have to sprinkle the cauliflower with a little more water as it cooks to stop it sticking to the pan. If there is still excess liquid when the cauliflower is cooked, simmer with the lid off until it dries out. Season with salt, to taste.

SERVES 4

Bhindi Masala

500 g (1 lb 2 oz) okra, about 5 cm (2 in) long
3 green chillies
3 tablespoons oil
1 teaspoon black mustard seeds
1 red onion, finely chopped

1 teaspoon ground cumin
1 teaspoon ground coriander
2 teaspoons garam masala (page 240)
1 teaspoon ground turmeric
4 garlic cloves, finely chopped

Wash the okra and dry with paper towels. Trim the tops and tails. Ignore any sticky, glutinous liquid that appears because this will disappear as the okra cooks.

Cut the chillies in half lengthwise, leaving them attached at the stalk, and scrape out any seeds. Heat the oil in a karhai or a deep, heavy-based frying pan, add the mustard seeds and onion and cook until the seeds pop and the onion is light brown. Add the cumin, coriander, garam masala and turmeric and cook until the popping stops.

Add the garlic, okra and the chilli to the pan, fry for 5 minutes, stir and cook for 2 minutes. Add 60 ml (2 fl oz/¼ cup) water, 1 tablespoon at a time, and stir to make a sauce. Season with salt, to taste. Simmer for about 15 minutes, or until the okra is cooked through and the sauce is thick and dry.

SERVES 4

Aloo Gobi

3 tablespoons oil
½ teaspoon black mustard seeds
½ onion, finely chopped
200 g (7 oz) potatoes, cut into cubes
¼ teaspoon ground turmeric
1 teaspoon ground cumin
1 teaspoon ground coriander

1½ teaspoons garam masala (page 240)
4 ripe tomatoes, chopped
1 large cauliflower (about 1.25 kg/2 lb 12 oz),
   cut into florets
2 cm (¾ in) piece of ginger
1 teaspoon sugar

Heat the oil in a karhai or a deep, heavy-based frying pan over low heat. Add the mustard seeds, cover the pan and wait for the seeds to pop. Add the onion and potato and fry until lightly browned.

Add the turmeric, cumin, coriander and garam masala to the pan and fry for a couple of seconds. Add the tomato and stir until the spices are well mixed. Add the cauliflower florets and stir until well mixed. Stir in the ginger, sugar and 125 ml (4 fl oz/½ cup) water, increase the heat to medium and bring to the boil. Reduce the heat, cover and simmer for 15 minutes, or until the vegetables are tender. Season with salt, to taste.

Uncover the pan and if the sauce is too runny, simmer it for another 1–2 minutes before serving.

SERVES 4

AVIAL

This mixed vegetable curry is from southern India where dishes often have more sauce to serve with rice, which is a staple there. Despite the chillies, this is quite a mild dish as the coconut and yoghurt sauce tones down the heat.

½ teaspoon ground turmeric
200 g (7 oz) carrots, cut into batons
200 g (7 oz) sweet potato, cut into batons
200 g (7 oz) green beans, topped and tailed
   and cut in half
50 g (2 oz) grated coconut (page 243)
5 cm (2 in) piece of ginger, grated

3 green chillies, finely chopped
1½ teaspoons ground cumin
420 ml (14 fl oz/1⅔ cups) thick plain yoghurt
   (page 246)
1 tablespoon oil
10 curry leaves

Bring 500 ml (17 fl oz/2 cups) water to the boil in a saucepan. Add the turmeric and carrot, reduce the heat and simmer for 5 minutes. Add the sweet potato and beans. Return to the boil, then reduce the heat and simmer for 5 minutes, or until the vegetables are almost cooked.

Put the grated coconut, ginger and chilli in a blender or pestle and mortar with a little water and blend or grind to a paste. Add to the vegetables with the cumin, season with salt and simmer for 2 minutes. Stir in the yoghurt and heat through.

For the final seasoning (tarka), heat the oil over low heat in a small saucepan. Add the curry leaves and allow to crisp. Pour the hot oil and leaves over the vegetables.

PICTURE ON PAGE 128

SERVES 4

Avial (recipe on page 127)

Spinach Kofta in Yoghurt Sauce

This is a typical Gujarati dish and is more substantial than some vegetarian dishes. You can eat the yoghurt sauce and the spinach kofta as separate dishes but they go very well together as in this recipe.

YOGHURT SAUCE
375 ml (13 fl oz/1½ cups) thick plain yoghurt
   (page 246)
4 tablespoons besan flour
1 tablespoon oil
2 teaspoons black mustard seeds
1 teaspoon fenugreek seeds
6 curry leaves
1 large onion, finely chopped
3 garlic cloves, crushed
1 teaspoon ground turmeric
½ teaspoon chilli powder

SPINACH KOFTAS
1 bunch English spinach (about 450 g/1 lb), leaves
   picked off the stems, or 500 g (1 lb 2 oz) frozen
   spinach, thawed and drained
170 g (6 oz/1½ cups) besan flour
1 red onion, finely chopped
1 ripe tomato, finely diced
2 garlic cloves, crushed
1 teaspoon ground cumin
2 tablespoons coriander (cilantro) leaves

oil, for deep-frying
coriander (cilantro) leaves (optional)

To make the yoghurt sauce, put the yoghurt, besan flour and 750 ml (27 fl oz/3 cups) water in a large bowl and whisk to a smooth paste. Heat the oil in a heavy-based saucepan or a deep frying pan over low heat. Add the mustard seeds, fenugreek seeds and curry leaves, cover and allow the seeds to pop for 1 minute. Add the chopped onion and cook for 5 minutes, or until soft and starting to brown. Add the garlic and stir for 1 minute, or until soft, then add the ground turmeric and chilli powder and stir for 30 seconds. Add the yoghurt mixture and bring to the boil, then reduce the heat and simmer over low heat for 10 minutes. Season with salt, to taste.

To make the spinach koftas, blanch the spinach in boiling water for 1 minute, then refresh in cold water. Drain and squeeze out any extra water by pressing the spinach between two plates. Finely chop the spinach. Combine with the remaining kofta ingredients and up to 60 ml (2 fl oz/¼ cup) of water, a little at a time, adding enough to make the mixture soft but not sloppy. If it becomes too sloppy, add more besan flour. Season with salt, to taste. (To test the seasoning, fry a small amount of the mixture and taste it.) Shape the mixture into balls by rolling it in dampened hands, using 1 tablespoon of mixture for each.

Fill a karhai or a heavy-based saucepan one-third full with oil and heat to 180°C (350°F), or until a cube of bread browns in 15 seconds when dropped in the oil. Lower the koftas into the oil in batches and fry until golden and crisp. Don't overcrowd the pan. Remove the koftas as they cook, shake off any excess oil and add them to the yoghurt sauce.

Gently reheat the yoghurt sauce and sprinkle with the coriander leaves if using.

SERVES 6

Matar Paneer

In the north of India, dairy products such as paneer are served regularly. This version of matar paneer is dry but it comes in various guises. If you don't want to make your own paneer, you can often buy it from Indian food shops or supermarkets.

225 g (8 oz) or ½ quantity paneer (page 245)
2 tablespoons ghee
50 g (2 oz) onion, chopped
200 g (7 oz/1⅓ cups) peas
½ teaspoon sugar
5 cm (2 in) piece of ginger, grated

2–3 green chillies, finely chopped
1 spring onion (scallion), finely chopped
½ teaspoon garam masala (page 240)
1 tablespoon chopped coriander (cilantro) leaves

Cut the paneer into 2 cm (¾ in) cubes. Heat the ghee in a karhai or heavy-based frying pan over medium heat and carefully fry the paneer until golden on all sides. Remove from the pan.

Lightly fry the onion in the same ghee, until it is softened and lightly golden. Remove the onion. Add 100 ml (4 fl oz) hot water and a pinch of salt to the ghee and simmer for 1 minute. Add the peas and sugar, cover and cook for 5–6 minutes, or until the peas are nearly cooked.

Add the fried onion, paneer, ginger, chilli and spring onion and cook for 2–3 minutes. Add the garam masala and coriander leaves. Season with salt, to taste.

SERVES 4

Far left: Carefully cut the paneer into small cubes.

Left: Fry the cubes of paneer until they are golden brown. Make sure the oil is hot enough, otherwise they may stick to the pan.

Punjabi Cabbage

½ onion, roughly chopped
1 garlic clove, roughly chopped
2.5 cm (1 in) piece of ginger, chopped
2 green chillies, seeded and chopped
80 ml (3 fl oz/⅓ cup) oil
1 teaspoon cumin seeds
1 teaspoon ground turmeric

500 g (1 lb 2 oz) green cabbage, finely shredded
1 teaspoon salt
½ teaspoon ground black pepper
2 teaspoons ground cumin
1 teaspoon ground coriander
¼ teaspoon chilli powder
1 tablespoon unsalted butter

Put the onion, garlic, ginger and chilli in a food processor and chop until finely chopped but not a paste, or chop together with a knife.

Heat the oil in a karhai or a heavy-based frying pan over low heat and fry the onion mixture until softened but not browned. Add the cumin seeds and turmeric to the pan and stir for 1 minute.

Mix in the cabbage, stirring thoroughly until all the leaves are coated in the yellow paste. Add the salt, pepper, cumin, coriander and chilli powder. Stir to coat the cabbage, then cook for 10 minutes with the pan partially covered, stirring occasionally until the cabbage is soft. If the cabbage starts to stick to the pan, add 1–2 tablespoons water. Stir in the butter and season with salt, to taste.

SERVES 4

Mooli Bhaji

The Asian radish, or mooli as it is also known, is much milder in flavour than its Western counterpart. It looks like a huge, white carrot and has crisp, juicy flesh. Bhaji is the name given to many vegetable dishes; it loosely means fried vegetables.

500 g (1 lb 2 oz) mooli
25 g (1 oz) grated coconut (page 243)
2 tablespoons oil
¼ teaspoon black mustard seeds

1 onion, chopped
¼ teaspoon ground turmeric
pinch of asafoetida
1 green chilli, finely chopped

Cut the mooli into batons. Heat a frying pan over low heat and dry-roast the coconut, stirring until it browns lightly.

Heat the oil in a karhai or heavy-based saucepan over low heat. Add the mustard seeds, cover and

allow to pop briefly. Add the onion and cook until lightly browned. Stir in the turmeric, asafoetida, chilli and the mooli until well mixed. Add 125 ml (4 fl oz/½ cup) water and simmer for 5–7 minutes, or until the mooli is cooked through and tender. Season with salt. Garnish with the coconut.

SERVES 4

SNAKE GOURD WITH YOGHURT

This recipe can be made using snake gourd, bitter melon or eggplant. Snake gourds are long, thin and sometimes curly vegetables that grow on vines. Growers sometimes tie a weight to the vegetable to straighten it as it grows.

250 g (9 oz) snake gourd
1 teaspoon ground turmeric
1 tablespoon oil
½ teaspoon black mustard seeds
½ teaspoon whole urad dal

2 dried chillies, cut in half
4 stalks of curry leaves
1½ red onions, finely chopped
250 ml (9 fl oz/1 cup) thick plain yoghurt (page 246)

Peel the snake gourd, slice in half horizontally and then slice diagonally into pieces about 1 cm (½ in) thick. Add the ground turmeric and a pinch of salt and rub into the pieces of gourd. Put the gourd in a sieve to allow any liquid to drain off.

Heat the oil in a karhai or heavy-based frying pan over low heat. Add the mustard seeds and urad dal. When the mustard seeds pop, add the chilli and the curry leaves and one-third of the onion. Cook until the onion is browned and softened. Add the snake gourd and toss over medium heat for about 10 minutes, or until the mixture looks dry and the gourd is tender. Remove from the heat.

Combine the yoghurt and remaining onion in a bowl and stir well. Fold the fried snake gourd into the yoghurt just before serving and season with salt, to taste.

SERVES 4

SAAG BHAJI

200 g (7 oz) small turnips, finely chopped
1 kg (2 lb 4 oz) mixed English spinach and amaranth
  leaves, finely shredded
½ teaspoon chilli powder

1 tablespoon ghee or oil
2 cm (¾ in) piece of ginger, grated
1 onion, finely chopped
1½ tablespoons lemon juice

Bring 125 ml (4 fl oz/½ cup) water to the boil in a large heavy-based saucepan over medium heat. Add the turnips, cook for 1–2 minutes, then add the spinach and amaranth. Stir in the chilli and a pinch of salt and cook for 2–3 minutes, or until almost all the water has evaporated. Mash well and remove from the heat.

Heat the ghee or oil in a heavy-based saucepan over low heat and fry the ginger and onion for 2–3 minutes. Add the mashed vegetable mixture and toss until well combined. Season with salt, to taste. Serve warm with a dash of lemon juice.

SERVES 4

Chapter 5

PULSES, RICE AND GRAINS

Pulses and rice are important staples in many regions. There are countless varieties of dal, and many different styles of pulao. Chickpeas also feature heavily in Indian cuisine.

Urad Dal

This type of lentil is used in the South to make dosas and idlis, but in Bengal, Gujarat and Rajasthan it is eaten regularly as a lentil stew. It is usually cooked with ginger, asafoetida and fennel seeds, an aromatic combination of spices.

250 g (9 oz) unskinned urad dal
¼ teaspoon ground turmeric
4 ripe tomatoes, chopped
1 small onion, roughly chopped
2 tablespoons oil
½ teaspoon cumin seeds

1 teaspoon fennel seeds
5 cm (2 in) piece of ginger, grated
2 dried chillies, broken into pieces
pinch of asafoetida
coriander (cilantro) leaves

Put the dal in a heavy-based saucepan with 1 litre (35 fl oz/4 cups) water and the turmeric, tomato and onion. Bring to the boil, then reduce the heat, cover and simmer for 40 minutes, or until the dal is cooked and feels soft when pressed between the thumb and index finger.

For the final seasoning (tarka), heat the oil in a small saucepan, add the cumin seeds and fennel seeds and allow to pop. Add the ginger, chilli and asafoetida and fry over low heat for 30 seconds. Pour into the hot dal and simmer for 5 minutes. Season with salt and garnish with coriander.

SERVES 4

The dal used for this recipe can be split but not skinned as shown here, or split and skinned.

ANDHRA-STYLE CHICKEN PULAO

1.5 kg (3 lb 5 oz) chicken or chicken pieces
1 kg (2 lb 4 oz/5 cups) basmati rice
3 onions, sliced
1/2 teaspoon salt
125 ml (4 fl oz/1/2 cup) oil
180 g (6 oz) ghee
4 cm (1 1/2 in) cinnamon stick
2 cardamom pods
3 cloves
2 star anise

2 stalks of curry leaves
2 cm (3/4 in) piece of ginger, grated
6 garlic cloves, crushed
4–6 green chillies, slit lengthwise
420 ml (14 fl oz/1 2/3 cups) buttermilk
4 ripe tomatoes, diced
185 ml (6 fl oz/3/4 cup) coconut milk (page 243)
1 litre (35 fl oz/4 cups) chicken stock
1 lemon, cut into wedges

If using a whole chicken, cut it into 16 pieces by removing both legs and cutting between the joint of the drumstick and thigh. Cut each of these in half through the bone with a cleaver or poultry shears (make sure there are no bone shards). Cut down either side of the backbone and remove the backbone. Turn the chicken over and cut through the cartilage down the centre of the breastbone. Cut each breast into three pieces and cut off the wings. Trim off the wing tips. Trim off any excess fat or skin from the pieces.

Wash the rice in a sieve under cold, running water until the water from the rice runs clear. Drain well. Put the sliced onion in a sieve, sprinkle with the salt and leave for 10 minutes. Rinse and pat dry.

Heat the oil and ghee over medium heat in a large, ovenproof 'degchi' (thick-based pot) or flameproof casserole. Add the cinnamon stick, cardamom and cloves and heat until they begin to crackle. Reduce the heat to low and add the star anise and curry leaves from one stem. Add the onion and cook

until golden brown. Add the ginger and garlic and cook until golden. Add the chicken pieces, increase the heat to medium and cook until the chicken is browned all over. Add the chillies, the remaining curry leaves, the buttermilk and some salt. Cook for 12 minutes, or until the chicken is cooked and the liquid is reduced by half. Add the diced tomato and the coconut milk and cook until the tomato is tender. Add the stock and bring to the boil.

Preheat the oven to 220°C (425°F/Gas 7). Add the drained rice to the chicken and stir it in well. Check the seasoning, adjust if necessary, and cook for 10 minutes, or until nearly all the liquid has been absorbed.

Remove the pot from the heat, cover with a clean wet cloth, then a tight-fitting lid, and put it in the oven for 15 minutes, or until the rice is cooked through. Serve hot with lemon wedges.

SERVES 8

Yoghurt Rice

This is a popular dish to prepare for taking on journeys as the dish is served cold and the acid in the yoghurt acts as a preservative. The flavours will not be as strong if you serve the rice straight from the fridge, so bring it back to room temperature.

2 tablespoons urad dal
2 tablespoons chana dal
225 g (8 oz) basmati rice
2 tablespoons oil
½ teaspoon mustard seeds

12 curry leaves
3 dried chillies
¼ teaspoon ground turmeric
pinch of asafoetida
500 ml (17 fl oz/2 cups) thick plain yoghurt (page 246)

Soak the dals in 250 ml (9 fl oz/1 cup) of boiling water for 3 hours. Wash the rice in a sieve under cold running water until the water from the rice runs clear. Drain.

Put the rice and 500 ml (17 fl oz/2 cups) water in a saucepan and bring to a rapid boil. Stir, cover, reduce the heat to a slow simmer and cook for 10 minutes. Leave for 15 minutes before fluffing up with a fork.

Drain the dals and pat dry with paper towels. For the final seasoning (tarka), heat the oil in a small saucepan over low heat, add the mustard seeds, cover and shake the pan until the seeds start to pop. Add the curry leaves, chillies and the dals and fry for 2 minutes, stirring occasionally. Stir in the turmeric and asafoetida.

Put the yoghurt in a large bowl, pour the fried dal mixture into the yoghurt and mix thoroughly. Mix the rice into the spicy yoghurt. Season with salt, to taste. Cover and refrigerate. Serve cold, but stand the rice at room temperature for about 10 minutes before serving. Serve as part of a meal. Yoghurt rice goes very well with meat dishes.

SERVES 4

Chole Chaat

220 g (8 oz/1 cup) chickpeas
2 tablespoons oil
½ onion, chopped
1 teaspoon ground coriander
1 teaspoon ground cumin

¼ teaspoon ground turmeric
1 teaspoon garam masala (page 240)
2 cm (¾ in) piece of ginger, grated
2 red chillies, finely chopped
200 g (7 oz) tin chopped tomatoes, drained

Put the chickpeas in a bowl with 2 litres (70 fl oz/ 8 cups) of water and leave to soak overnight. Drain well, then put the chickpeas in a large saucepan with 2 litres (70 fl oz/8 cups) water. Bring to the boil, spooning off any scum that rises to the surface. Reduce the heat, cover and simmer over low heat for 1–1½ hours, or until soft. It is important that the chickpeas are soft at this stage as they won't soften once the sauce is added. Drain, reserving the cooking liquid. Remove 6 tablespoons of the chickpeas and thoroughly mash them with a fork.

Heat the oil in a heavy-based saucepan over low heat and cook the onion until golden brown. Add the coriander, cumin, turmeric and garam masala and fry for 1 minute. Add the grated ginger, chilli, tomato and salt, to taste, and stir until well mixed. Add the chickpeas and their cooking liquid, along with the mashed chickpeas. Bring to the boil, then reduce the heat and simmer for 5 minutes. Serve at the start of an Indian meal, or as a side dish.

SERVES 4

Masala Rajma

225 g (8 oz) kidney beans
3 tablespoons oil
½ onion, finely chopped
2 Indian bay leaves (cassia leaves)
5 cm (2 in) cinnamon stick
2 garlic cloves, finely chopped

¼ teaspoon ground turmeric
½ teaspoon ground coriander
½ teaspoon ground cumin
½ teaspoon garam masala (page 240)
3 dried chillies
2 cm (¾ in) piece of ginger, grated

Soak the kidney beans overnight in 1.25 litres (44 fl oz/5 cups) water in a large saucepan. Drain, return the beans to the saucepan with 1.25 litres (44 fl oz/5 cups) water and bring to the boil. Boil for 15 minutes, then reduce the heat and simmer for 1 hour, or until the beans are tender. Drain, reserving the liquid.

Heat the oil in a heavy-based saucepan over low heat. Add the onion, bay leaves, cinnamon and garlic and cook until the onion is lightly browned. Stir in the turmeric, coriander, cumin, garam masala, chillies and ginger. Add the beans with enough liquid to make a sauce. Bring to the boil and cook, stirring, for 5 minutes. Season with salt.

SERVES 4

Sweet and Sour Chickpeas

500 g (1 lb 2 oz/2¼ cups) chickpeas
2 tablespoons oil or ghee
2 large red onions, thinly sliced
2 cm (¾ in) piece of ginger, finely chopped
2 teaspoons sugar
2 teaspoons ground coriander
2 teaspoons ground cumin

pinch of chilli powder (optional)
1 teaspoon garam masala (page 240)
3 tablespoons tamarind purée (page 246)
4 ripe tomatoes, chopped
4 tablespoons coriander (cilantro) or mint leaves,
  finely chopped

Put the chickpeas in a bowl with 2 litres (70 fl oz/8 cups) of water and leave to soak overnight. Drain well, then put the chickpeas in a large saucepan with 2 litres (70 fl oz/8 cups) water. Bring to the boil, spooning off any scum that rises to the surface. Reduce the heat, cover and simmer over low heat for 1–1½ hours, or until soft. It is important that the chickpeas are soft at this stage as they won't soften once the sauce is added. Drain.

Heat the oil in a karhai or heavy-based frying pan. Fry the onion until soft and brown, then stir in the ginger. Add the chickpeas, sugar, coriander, cumin, chilli, garam masala and a pinch of salt. Stir, then add the tamarind purée and tomato and simmer for 2–3 minutes. Add 500 ml (17 fl oz/2 cups) of water, bring to the boil and cook until the sauce has thickened. Stir in the coriander leaves. Serve with rotis (page 178).

PICTURE ON PAGE 148

SERVES 6

Dal Saag

225 g (8 oz) moong dal
2–3 tablespoons oil
1 teaspoon black mustard seeds
8 curry leaves
¼ teaspoon asafoetida
¼ teaspoon ground turmeric

1 teaspoon ground cumin
1 teaspoon ground coriander
3 cm (1¼ in) piece of ginger, grated
2 green chillies, seeded and cut into 1 cm (½ in) pieces
100 g (4 oz) English spinach leaves, roughly chopped
5 spring onions (scallions), finely chopped

Put the moong dal in a heavy-based saucepan, add 750 ml (27 fl oz/3 cups) of water and bring to the boil. Reduce the heat and simmer for 30 minutes, or until the moong dal are soft and breaking up. Add a little more water if necessary.

For the final seasoning (tarka), heat the oil in a saucepan, add the mustard seeds, cover and allow to pop. Stir in the curry leaves, asafoetida, turmeric, cumin, coriander, ginger and chilli, then pour into the cooked dal.

Stir in the spinach and spring onion and cook for about 2 minutes, or until the spinach is just cooked. Season with salt, to taste.

SERVES 4

Sweet and Sour Chickpeas (recipe on page 147)

IDIYAPPAM

In this dish from Kerala, the rice noodles are often made at home. However, this is quite labour intensive so we have used rice sticks or vermicelli as a substitute.

225 g (8 oz) rice sticks or vermicelli
80 ml (3 fl oz/⅓ cup) oil
50 g (2 oz/⅓ cup) cashew nuts
½ onion, chopped
3 eggs
150 g (6 oz/1 cup) fresh or frozen peas
10 curry leaves

2 carrots, grated
2 leeks, finely shredded
1 red capsicum (pepper), diced
2 tablespoons tomato sauce (ketchup)
1 tablespoon soy sauce
1 teaspoon salt

Soak the rice sticks in cold water for 30 minutes, then drain and put them in a saucepan of boiling water. Remove from the heat and leave in the pan for 3 minutes. Drain and refresh in cold water.

Heat 1 tablespoon oil in a frying pan and fry the cashews until golden, then remove. Add the onion to the pan, fry until dark golden, then drain on paper towels. Cook the eggs in boiling water for 10 minutes to hard-boil, then cool immediately in cold water. When cold, peel the eggs and cut into wedges. Cook the peas in a pan of boiling water until tender.

Heat the remaining oil in a frying pan and briefly fry the curry leaves. Add the carrot, leek and red capsicum and stir for 1 minute. Add the tomato sauce, soy sauce, salt and rice sticks and cook, stirring constantly to prevent the rice sticks from sticking to the pan. Serve on a platter and garnish with the peas, cashews, fried onion and egg.

SERVES 4

PULAO

Pulao or pilaf can be plain or a festive, elaborate dish with fruit, nuts and spices as found here. Rice dishes that reflect these flavours can be found as far afield as southern Russia, Persia and Morocco, a legacy of dishes travelling with conquerors and traders.

500 g (1 lb 2 oz/2½ cups) basmati rice
1 teaspoon cumin seeds
4 tablespoons ghee or oil
2 tablespoons chopped almonds
2 tablespoons raisins or sultanas
2 onions, thinly sliced
2 cinnamon sticks
5 cardamom pods

1 teaspoon sugar
1 tablespoon ginger juice (page 246)
15 saffron threads, soaked in 1 tablespoon warm milk
2 Indian bay leaves (cassia leaves)
250 ml (9 fl oz/1 cup) coconut milk (page 243)
2 tablespoons fresh or frozen peas
rosewater (optional)

Wash the rice in a sieve under cold, running water until the water from the rice runs clear. Drain the rice and put it in a saucepan, cover with water and soak for 30 minutes. Drain.

Place a small frying pan over low heat and dry-roast the cumin seeds until aromatic.

Heat the ghee or oil in a karhai or a heavy-based frying pan. Fry the chopped almonds and raisins until browned, then remove. Fry the onion in the same ghee until dark golden brown, then remove.

Add the rice, cumin seeds, cinnamon, cardamom, sugar, ginger juice, saffron and some salt, to taste, to the pan and fry for 2 minutes, or until aromatic.

Add the bay leaves and coconut milk to the pan, then add enough water to come about 5 cm (2 in) above the rice. Bring to the boil, cover and cook over medium heat for 8 minutes, or until most of the water has evaporated.

Add the peas to the pan and stir well. Reduce the heat to very low and cook until the rice is cooked through. Stir in the fried almonds, raisins and onion, reserving some for garnishing. Drizzle with a few drops of rosewater if you would like a more perfumed dish.

SERVES 6

TOOR DAL

In some parts of India it is common to combine a sweet and sour taste, particularly in lentil curries such as this one. Plan in advance when you want to make this dish as the dal has to be soaked before you cook it.

500 g (1 lb 2 oz) toor dal (yellow lentils)
5 x 5 cm (2 in) pieces of kokum
2 teaspoons coriander seeds
2 teaspoons cumin seeds
2 tablespoons oil
2 teaspoons black mustard seeds
10 curry leaves

7 cloves
10 cm (4 in) cinnamon stick
5 green chillies, finely chopped
½ teaspoon ground turmeric
400 g (14 oz) tin chopped tomatoes
20 g (1 oz) jaggery or 10 g (½ oz) molasses
coriander (cilantro) leaves

Soak the lentils in cold water for 2 hours. Rinse the kokum pieces, remove any stones and put the kokum in a bowl with cold water for a few minutes to soften. Drain the lentils and put them in a heavy-based saucepan with 1 litre (35 fl oz/4 cups) water and the pieces of kokum. Bring slowly to the boil, then simmer for about 40 minutes, or until the lentils feel soft when pressed between the thumb and index finger.

Place a small frying pan over low heat and dry-roast the coriander seeds until aromatic. Remove, then dry-roast the cumin seeds. Grind the roasted seeds to a fine powder using a spice grinder or a pestle and mortar.

For the final seasoning (tarka), heat the oil in a small pan over low heat. Add the mustard seeds and allow to pop. Add the curry leaves, cloves, cinnamon, chilli, turmeric and the roasted spice mix and cook for 1 minute. Add the tomato and cook for 2–3 minutes, or until the tomato is soft and can be broken up easily and incorporated into the sauce. Add the jaggery, then pour the mixture into the simmering lentils and cook for another 10 minutes. Season with salt, to taste. Garnish with coriander leaves.

SERVES 8

Test to see if the toor dal are cooked by gently squeezing them between your thumb and index finger. They should be soft.

Parippu

A dish that includes lentils of some sort is a must as part of any Indian meal. This recipe is from the South and is flavoured with coconut as well as a tarka of fried onion, cumin seeds, mustard seeds and curry leaves.

225 g (8 oz) masoor dal (red lentils)
1 onion, roughly chopped
1 ripe tomato, roughly chopped
50 g (2 oz) creamed coconut, mixed with 250 ml
  (9 fl oz/1 cup) water, or 250 ml (9 fl oz/1 cup) coconut
  milk (page 243)
2 green chillies, chopped
¼ teaspoon ground turmeric

½ teaspoon ground cumin
½ teaspoon ground coriander
2 tablespoons oil
1 teaspoon cumin seeds
½ teaspoon black mustard seeds
1 onion, very finely chopped
10 curry leaves

Put the lentils in a heavy-based saucepan with 500 ml (17 fl oz/2 cups) water. Add the roughly chopped onion, tomato, creamed coconut or coconut milk, chilli, ground turmeric, cumin and coriander, and bring to the boil. Reduce the heat and simmer, stirring occasionally, for 25 minutes, or until the lentils cook to a soft mush (masoor dal does not hold its shape when it cooks). If all the water has evaporated before the lentils are cooked, add 125 ml (4 fl oz/½ cup) boiling water.

For the final seasoning (tarka), heat the oil in a small saucepan over low heat. Add the cumin and mustard seeds, cover and allow the seeds to pop. Add the finely chopped onion and the curry leaves. Fry over low heat until the onion is golden brown. Pour the seasoned onion into the simmering lentils. Season with salt, to taste, and cook for 5 minutes.

SERVES 4

KALI DAL

Dal, which is both the name of the lentils, and in this case the dish, is part of the staple diet in India. This is a sumptuous version of a simple dish served with rotis in Sikh gurudwaras (temples). Kali means black and the gram in this dish have a black skin.

250 g (9 oz) whole black gram (sabat urad)
1 onion, roughly chopped
2 garlic cloves, roughly chopped
5 cm (2 in) piece of ginger, roughly chopped
1 green chilli, roughly chopped
125 ml (4 fl oz/½ cup) oil

2 tablespoons ground cumin
1 tablespoon ground coriander
2 teaspoons salt
¼ teaspoon chilli powder
3 tablespoons garam masala (page 240)
125 ml (4 fl oz/½ cup) cream

Put the whole black gram in a large, heavy-based saucepan, add 2 litres (70 fl oz/8 cups) water and bring to the boil. Reduce the heat and simmer for 1 hour, or until the dal feels soft when pressed between the thumb and index finger. Most of the dal will split to reveal the creamy insides. Drain, reserving the cooking liquid.

Blend the onion, garlic, ginger and chilli together in a food processor to form a paste, or finely chop them together with a knife.

Heat the oil in a frying pan and fry the onion mixture over high heat, stirring constantly, until golden brown. Add the cumin and coriander and fry for 2 minutes. Add the drained dal and stir in the salt, chilli powder and garam masala.

Pour 310 ml (11 fl oz/1¼ cups) of the reserved dal liquid into the pan, bring to the boil, then reduce the heat and simmer for 10 minutes. Just before serving, stir in the cream and simmer for another 2 minutes to heat through.

SERVES 6

LAMB BIRYANI

This is a rice and lamb dish in which both ingredients are cooked together in a sealed container. You can cook the lamb without browning it first and, in fact, this is the traditional method. However, browning the meat adds extra flavour.

1 kg (2 lb 4 oz) boneless lamb leg or shoulder,
    cut into 3 cm (1¼ in) cubes
8 cm (3 in) piece of ginger, grated
2 garlic cloves, crushed
2 tablespoons garam masala (page 240)
½ teaspoon chilli powder
½ teaspoon ground turmeric
4 green chillies, finely chopped
20 g (1 oz/⅔ cup) chopped coriander (cilantro) leaves
15 g (½ oz/¼ cup) chopped mint leaves
500 g (1 lb 2 oz/2½ cups) basmati rice

4 onions, thinly sliced
¼ teaspoon salt
125 ml (4 fl oz/½ cup) oil
125 g (5 oz) unsalted butter, melted
250 ml (9 fl oz/1 cup) thick plain yoghurt (page 246)
½ teaspoon saffron strands, soaked in 2 tablespoons
    hot milk

SEALING DOUGH
200 g (7 oz/1⅓ cups) wholewheat flour
1 teaspoon salt

Mix the lamb cubes in a bowl with the ginger, garlic, garam masala, chilli powder, turmeric, chilli, coriander and mint. Cover and marinate in the refrigerator overnight.

Wash the rice in a sieve under cold, running water until the water from the rice runs clear. Put the sliced onion in a sieve, sprinkle with the salt and leave for 10 minutes. Rinse and pat dry.

Heat the oil and butter in a large, heavy-based saucepan, add the onion and cook for 10 minutes, or until golden brown. Drain the onion through a sieve, reserving the oil and butter.

Remove the lamb from the marinade, reserving the marinade, and fry in batches in a little of the oil and butter until the lamb is well browned all over. Transfer to a 'degchi' (thick-based pot) or a flameproof casserole and add the browned onion, any remaining marinade and the yoghurt, and cook over low heat for 30–40 minutes, or until the lamb is tender.

In a separate saucepan, boil enough water to cover the rice. Add the rice to the pan. Return the water to the boil, cook the rice for 5 minutes, then drain well and spread the rice evenly over the meat. Pour 2 tablespoons of the leftover oil and ghee over the rice and drizzle with the saffron and milk.

To make the sealing dough, preheat the oven to 220°C (425°F/Gas 7). Make a dough by mixing the flour and salt with a little cold water. Roll the dough into a sausage shape and use to seal the lid onto the rim of the pot or casserole, pressing it along the rim where the lid meets the pot. Put the pot on the stovetop over high heat for 5 minutes to bring to the boil, then transfer it to the oven for 40 minutes. Remove the pot and break the seal of dough.

SERVES 6

BLACK-EYED BEANS WITH MUSHROOMS

Black-eyed beans or lobhia are sometimes called black-eyed peas. The earthy flavour of the lobhia combined with mushrooms and tomatoes makes this an excellent vegetarian main course. The dish is also suitable for serving as a side dish.

200 g (7 oz) black-eyed beans
400 g (14 oz) ripe tomatoes or 400 g (14 oz) tin
  chopped tomatoes
125 ml (4 fl oz/½ cup) oil
1 teaspoon cumin seeds
3 cm (1¼ in) cinnamon stick
150 g (6 oz) onion, chopped

4 garlic cloves, finely chopped
250 g (9 oz) mushrooms, sliced
2 teaspoons ground coriander
1 teaspoon ground cumin
½ teaspoon ground turmeric
¼ teaspoon cayenne pepper
2 tablespoons chopped coriander (cilantro) leaves

Put the black-eyed beans in a large saucepan with 1 litre (35 fl oz/4 cups) of water and bring to the boil. Cover and simmer for 2 minutes. Remove from the heat and stand for 1 hour. Alternatively, if you prefer, you can soak the black-eyed beans overnight in the cold water.

To peel the ripe tomatoes, score a cross in the top of each tomato. Plunge them into boiling water for 20 seconds, then drain the tomatoes and peel away from the cross. Roughly chop, discarding the cores and seeds and reserving any juices.

Bring the black-eyed beans back to the boil, then reduce the heat and simmer for 20–30 minutes, or until tender. Drain well.

Meanwhile, heat the oil in a karhai or deep, heavy-based frying pan or saucepan. Add the cumin seeds and cinnamon stick, let them sizzle for 10 seconds, then add the onion and garlic. Stir over medium heat until soft and just starting to brown. Add the sliced mushrooms and fry for 2–3 minutes. Add the tomato, ground coriander, cumin, turmeric and cayenne pepper. Cover and cook over low heat for 10 minutes.

Combine the black-eyed beans with the tomato and mushroom mixture and season with salt. Stir in the coriander leaves and simmer, uncovered, for 30 minutes.

SERVES 6

When the beans are soaked sufficiently, they will be creamy in colour and plump.

Khichhari

60 g (2 oz/¼ cup) toor dal (yellow lentils)
300 g (11 oz/1½ cups) basmati rice
3 tablespoons ghee
1 teaspoon cumin seeds
6 cloves
½ cinnamon stick

2 onions, finely chopped
2 garlic cloves, finely chopped
2 cm (¾ in) piece of ginger, finely chopped
1 teaspoon garam masala (page 240)
3 tablespoons lemon juice
1 teaspoon salt

Soak the dal in 500 ml (17 fl oz/2 cups) water for 2 hours. Wash the rice in a sieve under cold water until the water from the rice runs clear. Drain.

Heat the ghee in a heavy-based saucepan over low heat and fry the cumin seeds, cloves and cinnamon for a few seconds. Increase the heat to medium, add the onion, garlic and ginger and cook until they soften and begin to brown.

Add the rice and dal and toss to thoroughly coat in ghee. Add the garam masala, lemon juice, salt and 750 ml (27 fl oz/3 cups) boiling water. Bring to the boil, then reduce the heat to very low, cover tightly and cook for 15 minutes. Remove from the heat and gently fluff up with a fork. Cover the pan with a clean cloth and leave for 10 minutes. Fluff up again and season with salt, to taste.

SERVES 6

Prawn Pulao

200 g (7 oz/1 cup) basmati rice
300 g (11 oz) small prawns (shrimp)
3 tablespoons oil
1 onion, finely chopped
3 cm (1¼ in) cinnamon stick
6 cardamom pods

5 cloves
4 Indian bay leaves (cassia leaves)
1 stalk lemon grass, finely chopped
4 garlic cloves, crushed
5 cm (2 in) piece of ginger, grated
¼ teaspoon ground turmeric

Wash the rice in a sieve under cold running water until the water from the rice runs clear. Drain. Peel and devein the prawns, then wash thoroughly and pat dry with paper towels.

Heat the oil in a karhai or heavy-based frying pan over low heat. Fry the onion, cinnamon, cardamom, cloves, bay leaves and lemon grass until the onion is lightly browned. Stir in the garlic, ginger and turmeric. Add the prawns and stir until pink. Add the rice and fry over medium heat for 2 minutes. Add 500 ml (17 fl oz/2 cups) of boiling water and some salt and bring to the boil. Reduce the heat and simmer for 15 minutes. Remove the pan from the heat, cover tightly with a lid and then leave for 10 minutes. Lightly fluff up the rice before serving.

SERVES 4

Sevian Kheema

1 teaspoon cumin seeds
3 tablespoons ghee or oil
1 red onion, finely chopped
3 garlic cloves, crushed
2 cm (3/4 in) piece of ginger, grated

225 g (8 oz) minced (ground) lamb or beef
1 teaspoon ground black pepper
225 g (8 oz) sevian, broken into small pieces
3 tablespoons lime or lemon juice

Place a small frying pan over low heat, dry-roast the cumin seeds until aromatic, then grind to a fine powder using a spice grinder or pestle and mortar.

Heat 1 tablespoon ghee in a karhai or heavy-based frying pan and fry the onion, garlic and ginger for 3–4 minutes. Add the cumin, cook for 1 minute, then add the meat and cook for 8 minutes, or until the meat is dry, breaking up any lumps with the back of a fork. Season with the black pepper and salt, to taste, and remove from the pan.

Heat the remaining ghee and fry the sevian for 1–2 minutes. Add the meat and fry for 1 minute. Add 170 ml (6 fl oz/²/₃ cup) water and cook until the sevian are tender, adding more water if needed. The dish should be dry, so don't add too much at once. When cooked, sprinkle with the juice.

SERVES 4

Upama

2 tablespoons chana dal
4 tablespoons ghee or oil
75 g (3 oz/¹/₂ cup) cashew nuts
1 teaspoon black mustard seeds

15 curry leaves
¹/₂ onion, finely chopped
140 g (5 oz/1¹/₂ cups) coarse semolina
lime juice

Soak the dal in water for 3 hours. Drain, then put in a saucepan with 500 ml (17 fl oz/2 cups) water. Bring to the boil and cook for 2 minutes. Drain the dal, then dry in a tea towel. Brush some of the ghee on the cashew nuts and toast in a frying pan over low heat until they are golden.

Heat the remaining ghee in a heavy-based frying pan and add the mustard seeds and dal. Cook until the mustard seeds start to pop, add the curry leaves and onion and cook until the onion has softened. Add the semolina and toss to combine. When the semolina is hot and the grains are brown and coated in the oil, sprinkle with 500 ml (17 fl oz/2 cups) of boiling water, 125 ml (4 fl oz/¹/₂ cup) at a time, tossing and stirring after each addition, until all the water has been absorbed. Season with salt, to taste, and sprinkle with the lime juice and cashews.

SERVES 4

CHANA MASALA

Chana masala is served up by travelling vendors, in bazaars or on the streets of India, and eaten with puris. It is enjoyed at all times of the day as a snack or a light meal and makes a good accompaniment to any Indian meal.

250 g (9 oz) chickpeas
1 large onion, roughly chopped
2 garlic cloves, roughly chopped
5 cm (2 in) piece of ginger, roughly chopped
1 green chilli, chopped
170 ml (6 fl oz/²/₃ cup) oil
1 tablespoon ground cumin
1 tablespoon ground coriander
1 teaspoon chilli powder
pinch of asafoetida
2 tablespoons thick plain yoghurt (page 246)

2¼ tablespoons garam masala (page 240)
2 teaspoons tamarind purée (page 246)
½ lemon
3 green chillies, extra
¼ teaspoon ground black pepper
3 teaspoons salt
2 teaspoons chaat masala (page 240)
½ red onion, sliced into thin rings
2 cm (³/₄ in) piece of ginger, cut into thin strips
coriander (cilantro) leaves, roughly chopped (optional)

Put the chickpeas in a bowl with 2 litres (70 fl oz/ 8 cups) of water and leave to soak overnight. Drain well, then put the chickpeas in a large saucepan with 2 litres (70 fl oz/8 cups) water. Bring to the boil, spooning off any scum that rises to the surface. Reduce the heat, cover and simmer over low heat for 1–1½ hours, or until soft. It is important that the chickpeas are soft at this stage as they won't soften any further once the sauce is added. Drain, reserving the cooking liquid.

Blend the onion, garlic, ginger and chopped chilli to a paste in a food processor or very finely chop them together with a knife.

Heat the oil in a heavy-based saucepan and fry the onion mixture over medium heat until golden brown. Add the cumin, coriander, chilli powder and asafoetida, then stir for 1 minute. Add the yoghurt and stir for 1 minute. Stir in 2 tablespoons of the garam masala and then pour in 1.25 litres (44 fl oz/5 cups) of the reserved cooking liquid, a little at a time, stirring after each addition. Bring to the boil, then reduce the heat to a simmer.

Add the tamarind purée, lemon, whole chillies, chickpeas, pepper and the salt. Partially cover the saucepan and simmer for 30 minutes, then remove the lemon. Cook for another 30 minutes, or until all the liquid has reduced, leaving the softened chickpeas coated in a rich dark brown sauce.

Add the chaat masala and the remaining garam masala and stir in the raw onion rings, ginger and coriander leaves, if using.

SERVES 6

Chapter 6

BREADS

❖❖❖❖❖❖❖❖❖❖❖❖❖❖❖❖❖❖❖❖❖❖❖❖❖❖❖❖❖❖❖

*Bread, or roti, is eaten with every meal, and is used to scoop up liquid
or pick up pieces of meat, as well as forming edible wrappers or plates.
Choose from naan, parathas, chapatis, puris and idlis.*

PARATHAS

This fried unleavened bread is often eaten on special occasions. It is best cooked on a tava or iron griddle. You can use equal amounts of wholemeal and maida if you can't buy chapati flour.

200 g (7 oz/1⅓ cups) atta (chapati flour)
½ teaspoon salt

1 tablespoon oil or ghee
oil or ghee, for cooking and brushing

Sift the atta and salt into a bowl and make a well in the centre. Add about 170 ml (6 fl oz/⅔ cup) tepid water and the oil or ghee and mix to a soft pliable dough. Turn the dough out onto a lightly floured surface and knead for 5 minutes, then place in an oiled bowl, cover and allow to rest for 30 minutes. Divide the dough into six portions.

Roll each portion into a 15 cm (6 in) diameter circle. Using a pastry brush, cover the surface of each with a very thin coating of oil or ghee. Fold each paratha into a semicircle and brush lightly with oil or ghee. Fold into quarters and roll out each quarter to roughly three times its original size. Cover the rolled-out parathas with a cloth and cook them one at a time.

Heat a tava, griddle or a heavy-based frying pan over medium heat. Lightly brush the surface of the tava or griddle with oil. Remove the excess flour on each paratha by holding it in the palm of your hand and gently slapping it from one hand to the other. If you leave the flour on, it may burn.

Put a paratha on the tava and cook for 1 minute. Turn it over and cook for another minute, or until the surface has brown flecks. This cooking process should be quick to ensure the parathas remain soft. Repeat until all the parathas are cooked. Cover the cooked ones with a cloth.

Parathas must be served warm and can either be reheated in a microwave oven, or wrapped in foil and heated in a conventional oven for 10 minutes at 180°C (350°F/Gas 4).

MAKES 6

Far left: The ghee folded and rolled into the parathas will separate out the layers as they cook.

Left: Try to keep the shape neat as you roll.

Puris

Puris and puri crisps are simple to make even for a large group of people. The dough should be prepared ahead of time and allowed to rest. The oil should be hot so the puris puff up well, but not so hot that you burn the outside and undercook the inside.

325 g (11 oz/2²/₃ cups) maida or plain (all-purpose) flour
125 g (5 oz/1 cup) fine semolina

oil, for deep-frying

Mix the maida and semolina into a dough with 125 ml (4 fl oz/½ cup) water and knead well until firm. If necessary, add more maida to make the dough very firm. Cover and leave for 1 hour.

To make puris, knead the dough again, then divide into 12 balls. Roll each dough ball out to 1 mm (¹/₁₂ in) thick (not too thin), making a circle about 10 cm (4 in) in diameter.

Fill a karhai or a heavy-based saucepan one-third full with oil and heat to 180°C (350°F). Test the temperature by putting a small piece of the dough into the oil. If the dough rises to the surface in a couple of seconds, the oil is ready. Put a puri into the hot oil, then about 5 seconds after it rises to the surface, gently push it down, using the back of a spoon, to keep it submerged in the oil until

it puffs up – this will take about 5 seconds. Turn and cook until the other side is lightly browned. Remove from the oil and drain on a wire rack. The frying process should take 15–20 seconds for each puri. Continue until all the puris are cooked.

To make puri crisps, roll out the kneaded dough to 1 mm (¹/₁₂ in) thick (not too thin), cut out 4 cm (1½ in) diameter circles with a pastry cutter and set them aside on a tray.

Fill a karhai or a heavy-based saucepan one-third full with oil and heat until a small ball of dough will rise to the surface in a few seconds. Deep-fry the puri crisps in batches until golden and puffed. Drain on paper towels. If you have any remaining pastry, cut it into pieces and deep-fry them to make irregular-shaped crisps.

MAKES 12 LARGE OR 35 CRISPS

Right: Carefully lower one of the puris into the hot oil.

Far right: As the puris fry, they puff up and split into two very light layers.

CHAPATIS

Chapatis are the most basic form of unleavened bread. They should be cooked over a high heat to prevent them becoming tough. You can use equal amounts of wholemeal and maida if you can't buy chapati flour.

200 g (7 oz/1⅓ cups) atta (chapati flour)
½ teaspoon salt

100 g (4 oz) ghee or clarified butter

Sift the atta and salt into a bowl and make a well in the centre. Add about 170 ml (6 fl oz/⅔ cup) tepid water, enough to mix to form a soft, pliable dough. Turn the dough out onto a floured work surface and knead for 5 minutes. Place in an oiled bowl, cover and allow to rest for 30 minutes.

Put a tava or griddle, or a heavy-based frying pan over medium heat and leave it to heat up. Divide the dough into eight equal portions. Working with one portion at a time and keeping the rest covered, on a lightly floured surface roll out each portion to form a 15 cm (6 in) circle. Keep the rolled chapatis covered with a damp cloth while you roll them and cook them. Remove the excess surface flour on the chapati prior to cooking by holding the chapati in the palm of your hand and gently slapping it from one hand to the other. If you leave the flour on it may burn.

Place a chapati on the tava for 7–10 seconds to brown, then turn it over to brown the other side. Depending on the heat of the griddle, the second side should take about 15 seconds. Turn over the chapati again and, using a folded tea towel, apply gentle pressure to the chapati in several places to heat it and encourage it to puff up like a balloon. It is this puffing up process that gives the chapati its light texture. Smear the hot chapati with a little of the ghee or clarified butter, and leave it stacked and covered with a tea towel until all the chapatis are cooked.

MAKES 8

Far left: Slap the chapati backwards and forwards to get rid of any excess flour.

Left: Gently press the chapati with a tea towel to make it puff up as it cooks.

SAAG ROTI

A simple roti with a spinach base is not only interesting and tasty, but nutritious as well. Make it with some chopped browned onion for an aromatic alternative. You can use equal amounts of wholemeal and maida if you can't buy chapati flour.

200 g (7 oz) English spinach leaves, stalks removed
500 g (1 lb 2 oz/3⅓ cups) atta (chapati flour)
1 teaspoon salt

1 teaspoon ghee or oil
ghee or oil, for cooking

Briefly cook the spinach leaves in a little simmering water until just wilted, then refresh in cold water. Drain thoroughly, then finely chop. Squeeze out any extra water by pressing the spinach between two plates.

Sift the atta and salt into a bowl and make a well in the centre. Add the spinach, ghee and about 250 ml (9 fl oz/1 cup) tepid water and mix to form a soft, pliable dough. Turn out onto a floured work surface and knead for 5 minutes. Place in an oiled bowl, cover and allow to rest for 30 minutes.

Divide the dough into 20 balls. Working with one portion at a time and keeping the rest covered, on a lightly floured surface roll out each portion to a 12 cm (5 in) circle about 1 mm (¹⁄₁₂ in) thick.

Heat a tava, griddle or heavy-based frying pan and oil it lightly with ghee or oil. Place one roti on the tava or griddle and cook, covered with a saucepan lid (this will help keep it soft), for about 1 minute. Turn it over, cover again and cook the other side for 2 minutes. Check the roti a few times to make sure it doesn't overcook. The roti will blister a little and brown in some places. Remove the roti and keep it warm under a tea towel (dish towel) while you cook the remaining roti.

MAKES 20

Far left: Make sure that the spinach is evenly distributed throughout the dough.

Left: Cook the roti on one side, covered with a saucepan lid, before turning and cooking on the other side.

Idlis

220 g (8 oz) urad dal
100 g (4 oz/½ cup) rice flour (rava-idli)

1 teaspoon fenugreek seeds
1 teaspoon salt

Put the dal in a bowl, cover with water and soak for at least 4 hours, or overnight.

Drain the dal, then grind in a food processor or blender with a little water, to form a fine paste.

Combine the rice flour, fenugreek seeds and salt in a large bowl and mix in enough water to make a thick, pourable batter. Mix the batters together. Cover with a cloth and leave in a warm place for 8 hours, or until the batter ferments and bubbles. The batter will double in volume.

Pour the mixture into a greased idli mould, filling the cups almost full. Cover and steam the idlis over simmering water for 10–15 minutes, or until they are firm and puffed. Traditionally, the idlis are eaten with podi (page 199), or accompany dishes that have plenty of sauce.

PICTURE ON PAGE 180

MAKES 20

Quick Idlis

50 g (2 oz) chana dal
2 cm (¾ in) piece of ginger, finely chopped
310 g (11 oz/1¼ cups) thick plain yoghurt (page 246)
2 tablespoons oil
1 teaspoon black mustard seeds
10 curry leaves

1 green chilli, seeded and finely chopped
300 g (11 oz/2½ cups) fine semolina
25 g (1 oz) grated coconut (page 243)
¼ teaspoon baking soda
2 teaspoons salt

Put the dal in a bowl, cover with water and soak for at least 4 hours, or overnight. Drain and blend with the ginger, yoghurt and 170 ml (6 fl oz/⅔ cup) water in a food processor or blender, to form a loose paste.

Heat the oil in a frying pan, add the black mustard seeds, cover and shake the pan until the seeds start to pop. Add the curry leaves and chilli and fry for 1 minute. Add the semolina and grated coconut and stir for 2 minutes, or until they start to brown.

Mix both mixtures together and stir in the baking soda and salt. Leave for about 1 hour, or until the mixture thickens and becomes fluffy. Add enough water, about 625 ml (22 fl oz/2½ cups), to make a thick, pourable batter. Pour the mixture into a greased idli mould, filling the cups almost full.

Cover and steam the idlis over simmering water for 10 minutes, or until they are firm and puffed.

MAKES 16

Idlis (recipe on page 179)

Naan

Perhaps the most famous leavened bread from north India, traditionally this bread is cooked on the walls of a tandoor (clay oven). It is not easy to recreate the intense heat in a domestic oven so the texture is slightly different.

500 g (1 lb 2 oz/4 cups) maida or plain (all-purpose) flour
310 ml (11 fl oz/1¼ cups) milk
2 teaspoons (7 g/¼ oz) easy-blend dried yeast
 or 15 g (½ oz) fresh yeast
2 teaspoons kalonji (nigella seeds), (optional)

½ teaspoon baking powder
½ teaspoon salt
1 egg, beaten
2 tablespoons oil or ghee
185 ml (6 fl oz/¾ cup) thick plain yoghurt (page 246)

Sift the maida into a large bowl and make a well in the centre. Warm the milk in a saucepan until it is hand hot. If you are using fresh yeast, mix it with a little of the milk and a pinch of maida and set it aside to activate and go frothy.

Add the yeast, kalonji, baking powder and salt to the maida. In another bowl, mix the egg, oil and yoghurt. Pour into the maida with 250 ml (9 fl oz/ 1 cup) of the milk and mix to form a soft dough. Add the remaining milk if needed. Turn out onto a floured work surface and knead for 5 minutes, or until smooth and elastic. Put in an oiled bowl, cover and leave in a warm place to double in size. This will take several hours.

Preheat the oven to 200°C (400°F/Gas 6). Place a roasting tin half-filled with water at the bottom of the oven to prevent the naan from drying out.

Punch down the dough, knead it briefly and divide it into 10 portions. Using the tips of your fingers, spread out one portion of dough to the shape of a naan bread. They are traditionally tear-drop in shape, so pull the dough on one end. Put the naan on a greased baking tray. Bake on the top shelf for 7 minutes, then turn the naan over and cook for another 5 minutes. While the first naan is cooking, shape the next one. If your tray is big enough, you may be able to fit two naan at a time. Remove the cooked naan from the oven and cover with a cloth to keep it warm and soft while you cook the rest of the naan. Use the top shelf of the oven because the naan won't cook properly on the middle shelf. Refill the baking tray with more boiling water when necessary.

MAKES 10

Right: Knead the dough until it is very soft but not sticky.

Far right: Use the tips of your fingers to pull each portion of dough into a teardrop shape.

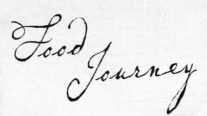

BREADS

In India, roti is the generic name for bread or bread-like accompaniments. There is a great variety and they are baked, grilled (broiled), roasted or fried. There is no rule regarding which type of roti goes with which dish.

Roti are popular all over India, especially in northern and central areas where wheat and grains are staples rather than rice. Although it is a common assumption that rice is part of every Indian meal, there are actually vast areas of India that don't have the right climate or terrain for rice growing. Therefore, these areas produce different grains and have a large repertoire of roti which commonly accompany meals.

In northern and central India, roti are eaten with every meal instead of rice. Throughout the rest of India, roti as well as rice are eaten with main meals every day. Roti function both as part of the meal and as a handy eating tool because they are used to scoop up the more liquid dishes including dal, or to pick up pieces of meat. Roti are also utilized as wrappers for grilled (broiled) meats, or as edible plates, with the accompaniments piled on top, at roadside stalls.

Roti made from wheat are generally cooked in one of four ways: on a tava (a flat, convex or concave griddle) without the use of fat, or on a tava using a little ghee or oil, or deep-fried in a karhai, or baked in a tandoor or oven. Each of the first three methods gives a different result using essentially the same unleavened dough. Sometimes, as for parathas, the dough is layered with ghee to give a flaky texture. At other times, it may be covered as it cooks to create a softer texture. Baked roti are made from leavened dough.

Unleavened roti cooked on a tava include chapatis, rumali, and phulkas (a type of chapati which is made to puff up by briefly cooking it on hot coals) as well as roti flavoured with spinach. Those cooked with fat are parathas. The most common deep-fried bread is the puri, which ranges from the tiny mouthfuls (gol goppas) used to make chaat, such as pani puri, to those bigger ones eaten with meals. Poppadoms are also a deep-fried accompaniment, though unlike the softer roti they are made from a dough of ground pulses and form a very thin, crisp disc with a bubbled surface.

Leavened breads rely on the intense, all-round heat of an oven or tandoor to make them rise and cook in minutes. The breads are stuck to the oven wall for a few minutes. They include naan, kulcha and sheermal. Baked breads are common to areas such as the Punjab, Hyderabad and Kashmir where ovens or tandoors (often communal) are commonly used. These ovens have been present in the Indus valley in northern India since the 2nd century BC and were introduced by the Moghuls. In other areas, baked breads are produced by restaurants as domestic kitchens do not have suitable ovens.

Other bread-like accompaniments include pancakes and cakes made of rice and gram, either steamed or cooked on griddles, such as idlis, appams and dosas.

Dosas

These are large, spongy, rice pancakes with a crisp surface. They are traditionally eaten with sambhar for breakfast. For the best result, rice flour that is specially made for making dosas should be sought out, as it is ground to the right consistency.

110 g (4 oz) urad dal
1 teaspoon salt

300 g (11 oz/1¾ cups) rice flour
oil or ghee, for cooking

Put the dal in a bowl and cover with water. Soak for at least 4 hours, or overnight.

Drain the dal, then grind with the salt and a little water in a food processor, a blender or a pestle and mortar to form a fine paste. Mix the paste with the rice flour, add 1 litre (35 fl oz/4 cups) of water and mix well. Cover with a cloth and leave in a warm place for 8 hours, or until the batter ferments and bubbles. The batter will double in volume.

Heat a tava or a non-stick frying pan over medium heat. Don't overheat it – the heat should always be medium. Lightly brush the tava or frying pan with oil. Stir the batter and then pour a ladleful into the middle of the griddle. Quickly spread it out with the back of the ladle or a palette knife, to form a thin pancake. Don't worry if it is not perfect, they are very hard to get exactly right. Drizzle a little oil or ghee around the edge of the dosa to help it crisp up. Cook until small holes start to appear on the surface and the edges start to curl. Turn over with a spatula and cook the other side. (The first dosa is often a disaster but it will season the pan for the following ones.)

Repeat with the remaining mixture, oiling the pan between each dosa. Roll the dosas into big tubes and keep warm. Dosas are often filled with potato masala filling (page 208) and served with chutneys, or with curries.

MAKES 20

Far left: Spread the dosa batter out as thinly as you can. This will take a little practice.

Left: When the edges start to curl, use a spatula to help turn the dosa.

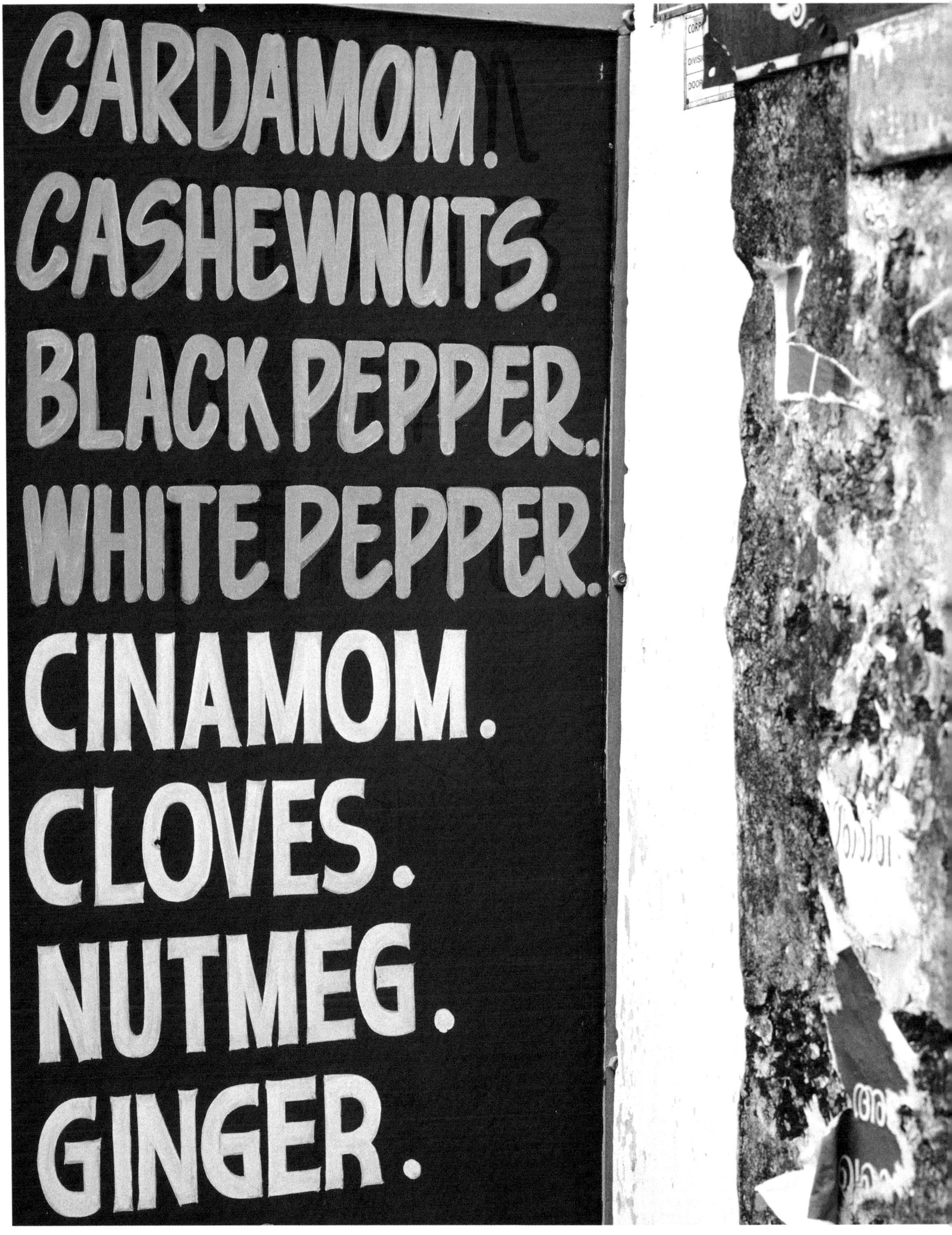
CARDAMOM.
CASHEWNUTS.
BLACK PEPPER.
WHITE PEPPER.
CINAMOM.
CLOVES.
NUTMEG.
GINGER.

ACCOMPANIMENTS

Chutneys, pickles, raitas and salads are as much a part of an Indian meal as the components that they accompany. They offer a contrast in texture and flavour and, in some cases, cooling relief from fiery spices.

LEMON PICKLE

Pickles are very much a part of an Indian meal. Although there are many varieties of commercially manufactured pickles available, a home-made one is far superior. Choose thin-skinned lemons for this if you can. You can also use Indian limes for this recipe.

500 g (1 lb 2 oz) thin-skinned lemons
1/2 teaspoon ground turmeric
2 tablespoons salt
1/2 teaspoon fenugreek seeds

1 teaspoon yellow mustard seeds
1/2 tablespoon chilli powder
2 tablespoons oil

Wash the lemons, place in a saucepan with 500 ml (17 fl oz/2 cups) water and the turmeric and bring slowly to the boil, skimming off any scum that rises to the top. Boil for 8 minutes, then remove from the heat and drain well.

Cut each lemon into eight sections and remove any pips. By this time, the flesh will have turned to a pulp. Sprinkle the lemons with the salt and pack them into a 500 ml (17 fl oz/2 cup) sterilized glass jar (wash the jar in boiling water and dry in a warm oven). Put the lid on tightly and keep the lemons in the jar for 1 week, turning the jar over every day. If the lid of the jar is too narrow to balance upside-down, store the jar on its side and roll it over every day instead.

Place a small frying pan over low heat and dry-roast the fenugreek seeds and mustard seeds until they are aromatic and starting to pop, shaking the pan occasionally to prevent them burning. Grind the seeds to a fine powder using a spice grinder or pestle and mortar.

Tip the lemons into a bowl and mix in the ground spices and chilli powder. Clean the jar and sterilize it again. Put the lemons and any juices back into the jar and pour the oil over the top to stop the top layer from discolouring. Store in a cool place, or in the refrigerator after opening.

MAKES 500 ML (17 FL OZ/2 CUPS)

Boiling the lemons will soften both the rind and flesh. Skim off any scum that appears on the surface of the water.

RADISH SALAD

Use the smallest radishes that you can find for this salad. Combining the radishes with peanuts gives a crunchy texture and hot flavour. It serves as a fresh-tasting accompaniment to most cooked dishes.

200 g (7 oz) small radishes
1 tablespoon oil
¼ teaspoon cumin seeds
¼ teaspoon black mustard seeds
pinch of asafoetida

¼ teaspoon ground turmeric
¼ teaspoon salt
1 tablespoon lemon juice
100 g (4 oz/⅔ cup) roasted peanuts,
    roughly chopped

Wash the radishes and top and tail them. Cut each radish into four or eight pieces.

Heat the oil in a small saucepan over medium heat, add the cumin and mustard seeds, then cover and shake the pan until the seeds start to pop.

Add the asafoetida, turmeric and salt to the pan, then remove from the heat, add the lemon juice and set aside to cool. Just before serving, arrange the radishes and the peanuts in a bowl, pour the dressing over the top and mix thoroughly.

SERVES 4

Mango Chutney

This is a wonderful mango chutney that is not too hot and is simple to make. It is one that is familiar to most people and goes with almost everything. Sweet chutney brings a contrasting flavour to savoury dishes and also goes well with poppadoms.

1 tablespoon oil
2 garlic cloves, crushed
1 teaspoon grated ginger
2 cinnamon sticks
4 cloves

½ teaspon chilli powder
1 kg (2 lb 4 oz) fresh or frozen ripe mango flesh,
    roughly chopped
375 ml (13 fl oz/1½ cups) clear vinegar
230 g (8 oz/1 cup) caster (superfine) sugar

Heat the oil in a medium heavy-based saucepan over medium heat, add the garlic and ginger and fry for 1 minute. Add the remaining ingredients and bring to the boil.

Reduce the heat to low and cook the chutney for 1 hour, or until the mango is thick and pulpy, like jam. It should fall in sheets off the spoon when it is ready. Season with salt, to taste, and more chilli powder if you wish. Remove the whole spices.

Pour the chutney into hot sterilized jars (wash the jars in boiling water and dry them thoroughly in a warm oven). Seal the jars and allow to cool completely. Store the chutney in a cool place, or in the refrigerator after opening.

MAKES 500 ML (17 FL OZ/2 CUPS)

Raita

A raita is similar to a pachadi, which is popular in southern India. Both have a yoghurt or curd base with varying vegetables or fruits added. A yoghurt dish is served with almost every Indian meal as a contrast to hot or spicy dishes.

450 g (1 lb) cucumbers
1 large, ripe tomato
310 ml (11 fl oz/1¼ cups) thick plain yoghurt (page 246)

2 teaspoons oil
1 teaspoon black mustard seeds
1 tablespoon coriander (cilantro) leaves (optional)

Grate the cucumbers and finely chop the tomato. Put the cucumber and tomato in a sieve and leave for 20 minutes to drain off all of the excess liquid. Transfer to a bowl, stir in the yoghurt and season with salt, to taste.

For the final seasoning (tarka), heat the oil in a small saucepan over medium heat, add the mustard seeds, then cover and shake the pan until the seeds start to pop. Pour over the yoghurt and serve sprinkled with the coriander leaves if you wish.

SERVES 4

Carrot Salad

Carrot salads are popular throughout India. In this one, the spices are heated in the oil in order for their flavour to permeate the dressing. This salad gets more flavoursome if it is allowed to stand for half an hour before serving.

1 tablespoon oil
¼ teaspoon black mustard seeds
¼ teaspoon cumin seeds
pinch of ground turmeric
¼ teaspoon salt

¼ teaspoon caster (superfine) sugar
1½ tablespoons lemon juice
500 g (1 lb 2 oz) carrots, grated
coriander (cilantro) leaves

Heat the oil in a small saucepan over medium heat. Add the mustard and cumin seeds, then cover and shake the pan until the seeds start to pop.

Add the turmeric, salt and sugar to the pan, then remove the pan from the heat and leave the spices to cool for 5 minutes.

Add the lemon juice to the spices, then toss the carrot through. Cover and leave for 30 minutes. Garnish with coriander leaves just before serving.

SERVES 4

Podi

Podi is a coarse powder used as a dip or as a seasoning. Eat it with idli or use it as a scatter seasoning for steamed vegetables or salads. This will make enough to last a long time so store it in a jar and use it as you need it (you can make half if you wish).

110 g (4 oz) urad dal
100 g (4 oz) chana dal
10 g (½ oz) dried chillies
75 g (3 oz/½ cup) sesame seeds

½ teaspoon sugar
½ teaspoon salt
1 tablespoon ghee

Place a small frying pan over low heat and dry-roast the urad dal, stirring constantly until brown. Remove from the pan and repeat with the chana dal, dried chillies and sesame seeds. Grind the roasted mixture to a powder with the sugar and salt, using a spice grinder or pestle and mortar.

Cool completely and store the mixture in a jar or an airtight container.

To serve, heat the ghee in a small frying pan and add 2 teaspoons of podi per person. Toss together until well mixed.

MAKES 220 G (8 OZ)

Fresh Coconut Chutney

Chutney made with fresh coconut is served with idlis and dosas for breakfast, or as a snack. The curry leaves and tamarind give a distinctive Indian flavour.

1 teaspoon chana dal
1 teaspoon urad dal
1/2 fresh coconut, grated
2 green chillies, seeded and finely chopped
1/2 teaspoon salt

1 tablespoon oil
1 teaspoon black mustard seeds
5 curry leaves
1 teaspoon tamarind purée (page 246)

Soak the chana dal and urad dal in cold water for 2 hours, then drain well.

Put the coconut, chilli and salt in a food processor and blend to a fine paste. If you don't have a food processor, either finely chop everything together with a knife or pound them in a pestle and mortar.

Heat the oil in a small saucepan. Add the mustard seeds and drained dals, then cover and shake the pan until they start to pop. Add the curry leaves and fry for 1 minute, or until the dal browns. Add these ingredients to the coconut with the tamarind and mix well.

SERVES 4

A grinding stone is used in India instead of a pestle and mortar. The grinding stone is rubbed back and forth over ingredients.

LACCHA

This speciality from Delhi is a tomato and onion accompaniment that is almost like a salad. It is easy to prepare and goes particularly well with tandoori meats and breads such as chapatis, puris or naan.

1 red onion, thinly sliced into rings
½ teaspoon salt
½ teaspoon cumin seeds
¼ teaspoon chilli powder

2 tomatoes, thinly sliced
450 g (1 lb) cucumbers, peeled and thinly sliced
3 tablespoons lemon juice

Mix the onion with the salt and leave in a sieve or colander to drain for 10 minutes. Rinse under cold water, then drain and put in a bowl.

Place a small frying pan over low heat and dry-roast the cumin seeds until aromatic. Grind the seeds to a fine powder using a spice grinder or pestle and mortar. Add the ground cumin and chilli powder to the onion and mix well.

Arrange the tomato slices on a plate and top with a layer of cucumber slices, then the onion mixture. Sprinkle with the lemon juice and season with salt and black pepper, to taste.

SERVES 6

Churri

1 teaspoon cumin seeds
10 g (½ oz/½ cup) mint leaves, chopped
15 g (½ oz/½ cup) coriander (cilantro) leaves,
    roughly chopped
2 cm (¾ in) piece of ginger, roughly chopped

2 green chillies, roughly chopped
310 ml (11 fl oz/1¼ cups) thick plain yoghurt (page 246)
310 ml (11 fl oz/1¼ cups) buttermilk
1 onion, thinly sliced

Place a small frying pan over low heat. Dry-roast the cumin seeds until aromatic, then grind to a fine powder in a spice grinder or pestle and mortar.

Chop the mint, coriander, ginger and chilli to a fine paste in a blender, or chop together finely with a knife. Add the yoghurt and buttermilk and a pinch of salt and blend until well mixed. Check the seasoning, adjust if necessary, then mix in the sliced onion and ground cumin, reserving a little cumin to sprinkle on top.

SERVES 4

Papaya Mustard Pickle

This is a wonderful pickle suitable for serving with roast lamb raan (page 97) or with pieces of roti and a quick dal curry or sambar. Make sure you use a green papaya and not a ripe one, otherwise the flesh will disintegrate when you cook it.

5 red chillies, seeded and chopped
1 large red onion, chopped
6 cm (2½ in) piece of ginger, grated
3 garlic cloves, chopped
60 g (2 oz) black mustard seeds
500 ml (17 fl oz/2 cups) clear vinegar
1 tablespoon oil

3 green chillies, seeded and chopped
200 g (7 oz) sugar
¼ teaspoon salt
¼ teaspoon ground turmeric
500 g (1 lb 2 oz) green papaya, cut into
    1 cm (½ in) cubes

Chop the red chilli, onion, ginger, garlic, mustard seeds and 125 ml (4 fl oz/½ cup) vinegar in a food processor or pestle and mortar to form a paste. The mustard seeds will not break up completely.

Heat the oil in a large heavy-based saucepan and cook the paste and the remaining vinegar until aromatic and reduced. Add the green chilli and sugar and stir until the sugar is dissolved. Add the salt, ground turmeric and papaya and simmer for 2 minutes, making sure the papaya stays firm.

Pour the pickle into sterilized jars (wash the jars in boiling water and dry them thoroughly in a warm oven) and leave to cool completely. Store in a cool place, or in the refrigerator after opening.

MAKES 1 LITRE (35 FL OZ/4 CUPS)

Carrot Pachadi

This delightful carrot side dish is similar to raita, pachadi being the southern Indian term for a yoghurt-based accompaniment. This goes particularly well with biryani and pulao but is suitable for serving with many other dishes as the yoghurt is soothing.

1 tablespoon oil
1 teaspoon black mustard seeds
2–3 dried chillies
¼ teaspoon asafoetida
1 stalk of curry leaves

625 ml (22 fl oz/2½ cups) thick plain yoghurt
  (page 246)
4 carrots, finely grated
coriander (cilantro) leaves

Heat the oil in a small saucepan over medium heat, add the mustard seeds and chillies, then cover and shake the pan until the seeds start to pop. Remove from the heat and immediately stir in the asafoetida and curry leaves.

Whisk the yoghurt to remove any lumps, then mix in the grated carrot. Add the spice mixture along with the oil, season with salt and garnish with the coriander leaves.

PICTURE ON PAGE 206

SERVES 4

Mango Salad

This is a delicious salad to be served with any meal. To choose ripe mangoes, check that they are only slightly soft when you touch them, then smell them to see whether they have that wonderful mango aroma.

300 g (11 oz) grated coconut (page 243)
2 dried chillies, seeded and chopped
1 tablespoon grated jaggery or soft brown sugar
300 g (11 oz) ripe mango flesh, cubed

1 tablespoon oil
½ teaspoon coriander seeds
½ teaspoon black mustard seeds
6 curry leaves

Put the grated coconut, chilli and jaggery or sugar in a blender and blend with enough water to make a thick, coarse paste. If you don't have a blender, crush everything together in a pestle and mortar, adding a little water as you go.

Transfer the paste to a bowl and toss the mango through. Season with salt, to taste, then refrigerate.

Heat the oil in a small frying pan over low heat and add the coriander seeds, mustard seeds and curry leaves. Cover and shake the pan until the seeds start to pop. Pour the oil and seeds over the mango mixture and stir.

SERVES 4

Carrot Pachadi (recipe on page 205)

Potato Masala

This filling is traditionally rolled in dosas to make masala dosa, which is served for breakfast or as a snack in southern India. However, it also makes an excellent spicy potato side dish.

2 tablespoons oil
1 teaspoon black mustard seeds
10 curry leaves
¼ teaspoon ground turmeric
1 cm (½ in) piece of ginger, grated

2 green chillies, finely chopped
2 onions, chopped
500 g (1 lb 2 oz) waxy potatoes, cut into 2 cm
    (¾ in) cubes
1 tablespoon tamarind purée (page 246)

Heat the oil in a heavy-based frying pan, add the mustard seeds, cover and when they start to pop add the curry leaves, turmeric, ginger, chilli and onion and cook, uncovered, until the onion is soft.

Add the potato cubes and 250 ml (9 fl oz/1 cup) water to the pan, bring to the boil, cover and cook until the potato is tender and almost breaking up.

If there is any liquid left in the pan, remove the lid and simmer until it evaporates. If the potato isn't cooked and there is no liquid left, add a little more water and continue to cook. Add the tamarind and season with salt, to taste.

SERVES 4

TAMARIND AND RAISIN CHUTNEY

2 teaspoons fennel seeds
250 ml (9 fl oz/1 cup) tamarind purée (page 246)
50 g (2 oz/¼ cup) pitted dates, chopped
30 g (1 oz/¼ cup) raisins
1 teaspoon chilli powder

180 g (6 oz) jaggery or soft brown sugar
1 tablespoon oil
½ teaspoon black mustard seeds
6 green chillies, slit in half and seeded but left whole

Place a small frying pan over low heat. Dry-roast the fennel seeds, stirring constantly until aromatic. Grind the fennel seeds to a fine powder using a spice grinder or pestle and mortar. Mix the ground fennel with the tamarind purée, dates, raisins, chilli powder, jaggery and a pinch of salt.

Heat the oil in a large, heavy-based saucepan over medium heat, add the mustard seeds, then cover and shake the pan until they start to pop. Add the date mixture and the chillies, bring to the boil and cook for 3 minutes, or until the mixture starts to thicken. Reduce the heat and simmer the chutney for 40 minutes, or until it is thick enough to fall off a spoon in sheets. Cool, then put in a sterilized jar (wash the jar in boiling water and dry it in a warm oven). Store in a cool place and refrigerate after opening.

MAKES 250 ML (9 FL OZ/1 CUP)

PINEAPPLE CHUTNEY

This quick and simple fresh pineapple chutney can be enjoyed as part of any main meal including meat and poultry or fish and seafood dishes. The acidity of the pineapple will cut through any rich dishes and make a refreshing contrast.

2 small or 1 large pineapple, slightly green
1 teaspoon salt
1 red onion, thinly sliced into half rings
4 red chillies, seeded and finely chopped
4 garlic cloves, finely chopped

2 teaspoons ginger juice (page 246)
30 g (1 oz/¼ cup) icing (confectioners') sugar,
  or to taste
125 ml (4 oz/½ cup) lime juice, or to taste

Peel the pineapple by cutting down the outside in strips. Remove any remaining eyes, then slice the flesh lengthwise and remove the tough core. Rub the pineapple with the salt and leave it to sit for a few minutes in a colander to draw out some of the juices. Rinse, then cut into small chunks and drain well on paper towels.

Mix all the ingredients together in a bowl, adding enough sugar, lime juice, pepper and salt to achieve a balanced flavour. Chill before serving.

SERVES 6

Mint and Coriander Chutney

This refreshing mint and coriander chutney is perfect for serving with samosas, but can be served with just about any Indian meal.

30 g (1 oz/1½ cups) mint leaves
30 g (1 oz/1 cup) coriander (cilantro) leaves
1 green chilli
1 tablespoon tamarind purée (page 246)

½ teaspoon salt
1½ teaspoons sugar
3 tablespoons thick plain yoghurt (page 246), (optional)

Wash the mint leaves and coriander leaves. Discard any tough stalks but keep the young soft ones for flavour. Blend all the ingredients in a blender or food processor, or chop everything finely with a knife and pound it together in a pestle and mortar. Taste the chutney and add more salt if necessary. If you want a creamier, milder chutney, stir in the thick yoghurt.

SERVES 4

Sweet Tomato Chutney

This is an easy store-cupboard chutney. It is an especially handy recipe if you have an abundance of very ripe tomatoes (you will need about 800 g/1 lb 12 oz peeled fresh tomatoes). If you can't find clear vinegar at Indian food shops, use white vinegar.

8 garlic cloves, roughly chopped
5 cm (2 in) piece of ginger, roughly chopped
2 x 400 g (14 oz) tins chopped tomatoes
310 ml (11 fl oz/1¼ cups) clear vinegar
350 g (12 oz) jaggery or soft brown sugar

2 tablespoons sultanas
2 teaspoons salt
¾ teaspoon cayenne pepper
chilli powder (optional)

Blend the garlic, ginger and half the tomatoes in a blender or food processor until smooth. If you don't have a blender or food processor, crush the garlic, grate the ginger and push the tomatoes through a sieve before mixing them all together.

Put the remaining tomatoes, the vinegar, sugar, sultanas and salt in a large, heavy-based saucepan. Bring to the boil and add the garlic and ginger mixture. Reduce the heat and simmer gently for 1½–1¾ hours, stirring occasionally, until it is thick enough to fall off a spoon in sheets. Make sure the mixture doesn't catch on the base of the pan.

Add the cayenne pepper. For a hotter chutney, add a little chilli powder. Leave to cool, then pour into sterilized jars (wash the jars in boiling water and dry them thoroughly in a warm oven) and store in a cool place, or in the refrigerator after opening.

MAKES 500 ML (17 FL OZ/2 CUPS)

Chapter 8

SWEETS AND DRINKS

Sweets are both a part of everyday life and bought as gifts or religious offerings. Cold drinks bring welcome refreshment, while hot drinks provide an excuse to stop and talk as the world passes by.

KULFI

Young and old take great delight in these flavoured ices that are sold in India at roadside stalls. They are not generally made in households as they are time consuming.

2 litres (70 fl oz/8 cups) milk
10 cardamom pods, lightly crushed
6 tablespoons sugar
15 g (½ oz) almonds, blanched and finely chopped

15 g (½ oz) unsalted pistachio nuts, skinned and
    finely chopped
edible silver leaf (varak), (optional)

Put the milk and cardamom pods in a heavy-based saucepan and bring to the boil. Reduce the heat to low and simmer, stirring frequently, for 2 hours, or until the milk has reduced to a third of the original amount, about 750 ml (27 fl oz/3 cups). Whenever a thin skin forms on top, stir it back in.

Add the sugar to the pan, simmer for 5 minutes, then strain into a shallow plastic freezer box. Add the almonds and half the pistachios, then cool. Put twelve 80 ml (3 fl oz/⅓ cup) kulfi moulds or dariole moulds in the freezer to chill.

Place the kulfi mixture in the freezer and every 20 minutes, using electric beaters or a fork, give the ice cream a good stir to break up the ice crystals. When the mixture is quite stiff, divide it among the moulds and freeze until hardened completely. Dip the moulds in hot water and turn out the kulfi. Sprinkle with the remaining pistachios and decorate with silver leaf.

MAKES 12

Far left: Kulfi are made in specially shaped moulds. When the mixture has hardened, fill the conical moulds.

Left: The moulds have a lid that is screwed on before freezing the kulfi.

Salt Lassi

Lassis are a very popular drink in India. They are made by blending yoghurt with a flavouring, which can be either salty or sweet. Both these versions are cooling, refreshing and perfect to drink with a curry.

1 teaspoon cumin seeds
625 ml (22 fl oz/2½ cups) thick plain yoghurt (page 246)

½ teaspoon salt

Place a small frying pan over low heat and dry-roast the cumin seeds until browned and aromatic.

Blend the cumin seeds (reserve a few for garnish) by hand or in a blender with the yoghurt, salt and

310 ml (11 fl oz/1¼ cups) water. If you would like the lassi a little colder, add about eight ice cubes to the blender, or stir them into the blended lassi. Serve in tall glasses, garnished with the reserved cumin seeds.

SERVES 4

Mango Lassi

500 g (1 lb 2 oz) ripe mango
250 ml (9 fl oz/1 cup) chilled milk

250 ml (9 fl oz/1 cup) thick plain yoghurt (page 246)

Chop the mango to a pulp using a knife or blender, add a pinch of salt and push through a nylon sieve with the back of a spoon. Discard any fibres. The remaining syrup should be thick but should not contain any stringy bits of pulp. Refrigerate the mango until cold.

Blend the mango with the milk and yoghurt, either by hand or in a blender. If you would like the lassi

a little colder, add about eight ice cubes to the blender, or stir them into the blended lassi.

If you want to use green unripe mangoes, cook them with 220 g (8 oz/1 cup) sugar and a little water and add 500 ml (17 fl oz/2 cups) milk to the lassi, instead of yoghurt and milk.

SERVES 4

Apricots in Cardamom Syrup

A Kashmiri speciality best made from dried Kashmiri apricots, which have lots of flavour. The silver leaf makes this a special dessert but does not have to be used. It can be served with thick cream or yoghurt to temper the sweetness.

300 g (11 oz/1²/₃ cups) dried apricots
3 tablespoons caster (superfine) sugar
3 tablespoons slivered, blanched almonds
1 cm (½ in) piece of ginger, sliced

4 cardamom pods
1 cinnamon stick
4 pieces edible silver leaf (varak), (optional)

Soak the apricots in a large saucepan with 750 ml (27 fl oz/3 cups) water for 4 hours, or until plump.

Add the sugar, blanched almonds, ginger slices, cardamom pods and cinnamon to the apricots and bring slowly to the boil, stirring until the sugar has dissolved. Reduce the heat to a simmer and cook until the liquid has reduced by half and formed a thick syrup. Pour into a bowl, then refrigerate.

Serve in small bowls with a piece of silver leaf for decoration. To do this, invert the piece of backing paper over each bowl. As soon as the silver leaf touches the apricots it will come away from the backing and stick to them.

SERVES 4

GULAB JAMUN

Literally translated to mean rose-flavoured plum, gulab jamun is an extremely popular Indian sweet. A pinch of cardamom can be added to the dough for extra flavour.

SYRUP
440 g (16 oz/2 cups) sugar
4–5 drops rosewater

GULAB JAMUN
100 g (4 oz/1 cup) low-fat powdered milk
2 tablespoons self-raising flour

2 teaspoons fine semolina
2 tablespoons ghee
4 tablespoons milk, to mix
24 pistachio nuts (optional)
oil, for deep-frying

To make the syrup, put the sugar in a large heavy-based saucepan with 850 ml (30 fl oz/3⅓ cups) of water. Stir over low heat to dissolve the sugar, then increase the heat and boil for 3 minutes. Stir in the rosewater and remove from the heat.

To make the gulab jamun, combine the powdered milk, flour, semolina and ghee in a bowl. Add just enough milk to make a soft dough and mix until smooth. Divide the dough into 24 portions. If you are using pistachio nuts, press each piece of dough in the centre to make a hole, fill with a pistachio, then roll into a ball. If you are not using pistachios, just roll each piece into a ball.

Fill a karhai or deep saucepan one-third full with oil. Heat the oil to 150°C (300°F), or until a cube of bread browns in 30 seconds when dropped into the oil. Fry the balls until golden brown all over. Remove with a slotted spoon and transfer to the syrup. When all the balls are in the syrup, bring the syrup to boiling point, then remove from the heat. Set aside to cool, and serve the gulab jamun at room temperature.

MAKES 24

Right: Roll the dough into smooth balls.

Far right: When the balls have fried to a deep golden brown, add them to the flavoured sugar syrup.

Food Journey

SWEETS

A fondness for sweets (mithai) is common throughout India. Unlike in the West, there is no distinction between sweets and desserts. Both are sold at sweet shops and neither is commonly eaten at the end of a meal. Instead, mithai represent a form of greeting, are used as religious offerings and are symbolic of hospitality.

Mithai vary regionally and many places have a sweet speciality. In areas such as Bengal, the sweet capital of India, towns and small villages have their own particular varieties. Common sweets such as barfi and laddu are available everywhere.

Sweets generally fit into categories based on their main ingredient, shape, or method of production. Barfi are types of fudge. Their name comes from the Persian word for snow and in their original form they were probably all white. Barfi are based on khoya, a milk product, and are very sweet. Those with ground nuts or flour in them have a grainier texture than the plain milk (dhoodh) versions.

Sandesh, based on chenna mixed with sugar, are one of the finest Indian sweets. The name means 'news' and the sweets were originally sent to friends by messenger as a means of enquiring after them. Sandesh can be made in a variety of textures and flavours and they are often pressed into decorative moulds. As a speciality of Bengal, sandesh are made into shapes such as conch shells or fish, which are representative of that area.

Halva have a thick, pudding-like texture and are based on ingredients such as semolina, grated carrot, besan flour and pulses. Sweet-makers in India are called 'halvais'.

Laddu are named for their ball shape rather than their ingredients. They are made with a besan flour or coarse flour dough which is pressed into patties, deep-fried, then crumbled and shaped into balls with sugar, ghee, spices and nuts. There are many variations, some of which are made with puffed rice mixed with sugar and often nuts.

Deep-fried sweets are fried in oil and then soaked in sugar syrup such as jalebi and imarti (loops of orange dough).

Milk-based sweets and desserts range from the Bengali specialities of rossogollas and kheer (rice pudding) to southern dishes such as payasam (sago or sevian puddings).

Indian sweets are required not only to taste good but also to look fabulous. They are often coloured with pink, yellow or green, studded with nuts or sultanas, or covered with a gossamer-fine layer of gold or silver leaf (varak). Though everyday sweets are not as fancy, those sold at festival times are made more elaborate with extra decorations.

Saffron, cardamom, rose essence, pistachio, kewra (pandanus), khus (fragrant grass), coconut and almond are the most common flavours of sweets. Unrefined sugars such as gur or jaggery also add flavour and are often preferred to refined sugar.

ROSSOGOLLAS

Kolkata (Calcutta) is the city where the best Bengali sweets can be found. Rossogollas or rasgullas are sweetened milk balls in syrup, said to have been invented by an old firm, K.C. Das, which specializes in sweets. Make the chenna before you start.

1 quantity chenna (page 245)
3 tablespoons chopped nuts (optional)

SYRUP
1 kg (2 lb 4 oz/4½ cups) sugar
3 tablespoons milk
rosewater (optional)

Divide the chenna dough into 30 portions and roll each into a ball. If you are using the nuts, make a hollow in each ball, add a few chopped nuts to the centre, then re-roll as a ball.

Make a thin syrup by combining the sugar with 1.5 litres (52 fl oz/6 cups) water in a heavy-based saucepan and simmering the mixture over low heat until it is slightly thickened. The syrup should feel sticky and greasy. Add the milk to the boiling syrup to clarify it – this will force any scum to rise to the surface. Skim off the scum with a spoon.

Drop the rossogollas into the clean boiling syrup, then reduce the heat and simmer for 10 minutes, or until they float to the surface. Sprinkle a little water on the syrup every 2 minutes to stop it from reducing too much and foaming.

Remove from the heat and leave the rossogollas to cool in the syrup. If you would like a rose flavour, add a few drops of rosewater. Keep the rossogollas refrigerated until required. Serve with a little of the syrup poured over them.

SERVES 6

Far left: Make a dent in each ball and fill it with nuts before smoothing the balls into shape.

Left: Gently poach the rossogollas in the sugar syrup.

Kheer

This is the Indian version of rice pudding and is made on the stovetop instead of in the oven. It is exotically delicious, rich and creamy, with the cardamom and almonds giving it a distinctive texture and flavour.

150 g (6 oz/³/₄ cup) basmati rice
20 cardamom pods
2.5 litres (87 fl oz/10 cups) milk

30 g (1 oz/¹/₃ cup) flaked almonds
165 g (6 oz/³/₄ cup) sugar
30 g (1 oz/¹/₄ cup) sultanas

Wash the rice, then soak for 30 minutes in cold water. Drain well. Remove the seeds from the cardamom pods and lightly crush them in a spice grinder or pestle and mortar.

Bring the milk to the boil in a large heavy-based saucepan and add the rice and cardamom. Reduce the heat and simmer the rice, stirring occasionally, for 1¹/₂–2 hours, or until creamy.

Dry-fry the almonds in a frying pan over medium heat for a few minutes. Add the sugar, almonds and sultanas to the creamy rice, reserving some of the almonds and sultanas for garnishing. Mix, then divide among serving bowls and garnish with the reserved almonds and sultanas. Serve warm.

SERVES 6

Carrot Halva

This is a very simple Indian sweet. The only secret to making it look authentic is to use really bright-orange carrots to give a good colour. Carrot halva is traditionally made in the winter months and is best eaten hot with a dollop of cream.

1 kg (2 lb 4 oz) carrots, grated
1 litre (35 fl oz/4 cups) milk
100 g (4 oz) ghee
230 g (8 oz/1 cup) caster (superfine) sugar

80 g (3 oz/²/₃ cup) raisins
1 teaspoon cardamom seeds, finely ground
50 g (2 oz/¹/₂ cup) slivered almonds
ground cardamom

Put the grated carrot and milk in a heavy-based saucepan over low heat and bring to a simmer. Cook, stirring, until the carrot is tender and the milk has evaporated. This must be done slowly or the mixture will burn. Add the ghee and cook until the carrot starts to brown.

Add the sugar and cook until the mixture is thick and dry. Add the raisins, cardamom and almonds. Serve hot in small bowls, with thick cream or ice cream, and sprinkle with a little ground cardamom.

SERVES 8

SHRIKHAND

This is yet another milk-based recipe. It is traditionally made by straining yoghurt and flavouring it with saffron and cardamom to give a thick, rich, creamy dessert.

½ teaspoon saffron strands
3 cardamom pods
250 ml (9 fl oz/1 cup) thick plain yoghurt (page 246)

3 tablespoons caster (superfine) sugar
a few toasted flaked almonds

Soak the saffron in 1 teaspoon of boiling water. Remove the cardamom seeds from the pods and coarsely crush them in a spice grinder or pestle and mortar.

Put the yoghurt, sugar, cardamom and saffron in a bowl and beat until well mixed. Divide among four bowls and refrigerate before serving. Serve with toasted almonds sprinkled on top.

SERVES 4

CASHEW NUT BARFI

500 g (1 lb 2 oz) cashew nuts
6 cardamom pods
200 g (7 oz/2 cups) powdered milk
2 tablespoons ghee or butter

¼ teaspoon ground cloves
230 g (8 oz/1 cup) caster (superfine) sugar
2 sheets edible silver leaf (varak), (optional)

Place a small frying pan over low heat and dry-roast the cashew nuts until browned all over. Cool and then chop in a food processor or with a knife. Remove the cardamom seeds from the pods and crush them in a spice grinder or pestle and mortar. Line a 26 x 17 cm (10½ x 7 in) baking tin with baking paper.

Combine the milk powder and cashew nuts in a large bowl and rub in the ghee until completely mixed in. Stir in the cardamom and cloves.

Combine the sugar and 250 ml (9 fl oz/1 cup) of water in a heavy-based saucepan and heat over low heat until the sugar melts. Bring to the boil and then reduce the heat and simmer for 5–7 minutes to make a sugar syrup. Quickly stir the syrup into the cashew mixture (if you leave it too long it will stiffen), spread the mixture into the baking tin and smooth the top with a buttered spatula. Place the silver leaf on top by inverting the sheets onto the surface and peeling off the paper backing. Leave to cool, then slice into diamond shapes. Serve cold.

SERVES 12

Falooda

Sweet drinks, Indian Muslim in origin, are often drunk during the month-long Ramadan fast. In this rosewater drink, the sugar is an energy source that is highly recommended while fasting.

ROSE SYRUP
220 g (8 oz/1 cup) sugar
2 teaspoons rosewater, or to taste
pink food colouring

FALOODA
2 teaspoons agar-agar
yellow food colouring

30 g (1 oz) basil seeds
1 tablespoon icing (confectioners') sugar
1 litre (35 fl oz/4 cups) milk, chilled
6 tablespoons ice cream or thick (double/heavy) cream
pistachios, chopped (optional)
almonds, chopped (optional)
mint leaves (optional)

To make the rose syrup, put the sugar and 250 ml (9 fl oz/1 cup) of water in a large, heavy-based saucepan, bring to the boil and boil for 2 minutes. Add rosewater, to taste, and enough colouring to make a pink syrup. Cool.

To prepare the falooda, dissolve the agar-agar in 250 ml (9 fl oz/1 cup) of boiling water in a small saucepan. Cook over medium heat for 15 minutes, stirring constantly. Add a little yellow colouring and then pour into a large, flat dish. Refrigerate until set, turn out onto a board and slice into thin strips (thin enough to be sucked up a straw).

Soak the basil seeds in a little water for 1 hour, then drain. Stir the icing sugar into the milk.

To prepare six glasses of falooda, pour 2 tablespoons rose syrup into each large glass. Add a helping of falooda and 2–3 teaspoons basil seeds to each and top with the chilled milk and 1 tablespoon cream or ice cream. Garnish with nuts and mint leaves if you wish.

SERVES 6

Masala Coffee

This is the Keralan cappuccino, a traditional way of making coffee, seen on every street corner. The coffee-maker, often clad in a checked sarong, is the focus of the village after work and coffee is a must for stimulating talk as the world passes by.

500 ml (17 fl oz/2 cups) milk
2 tablespoons sugar
2 cm (3/4 in) piece of ginger
2 tablespoons freshly ground Keralan or other coffee

5 cardamom seeds, pounded
1 cinnamon stick
cocoa powder

Put the milk and sugar in a heavy-based saucepan, bring to the boil over low heat and then keep at a low simmer.

Dry-roast the ginger under a grill (broiler) for 1 minute on each side, then pound it a little in a pestle and mortar to crush it and release the juices. Add the ginger to the milk along with the coffee, cardamom and cinnamon. Cover and allow the flavourings to steep in the heat for 3 minutes.

Strain off the dregs (the easiest way is to put the whole lot through a coffee plunger or a very fine strainer), then pour the coffee from one pitcher to another in a steady stream. You need to hold the pitchers far apart and repeat the process until the coffee begins to froth. Serve hot, garnished with a sprinkling of cocoa.

SERVES 4

Masala Chai

2 cm (3/4 in) piece of ginger
5 cm (2 in) cinnamon stick
4 peppercorns
3 cloves

3 cardamom pods
1 tablespoon black Indian tea
250 ml (9 fl oz/1 cup) milk
3 tablespoons sugar

Dry-roast the ginger under a grill (broiler) for 1 minute on each side. Put the ginger, cinnamon, peppercorns, cloves and cardamom in a pestle and mortar or spice grinder and roughly crush them. Put the spice mixture, tea and milk in a saucepan with 1 litre (35 fl oz/4 cups) of water and bring to the boil. Leave for 3 minutes, then add the sugar.

Strain off the dregs (the easiest way is to put the whole lot through a coffee plunger or a very fine strainer), then pour the tea from one pitcher to another in a steady stream. You need to hold the pitchers far apart and repeat the process until the tea begins to froth. Serve hot, in glasses.

SERVES 6

ALMOND SARBAT

12 cardamom pods
250 g (9 oz/2½ cups) freshly ground almonds
1 kg (2 lb 4 oz/4½ cups) sugar

natural almond extract, to taste
5–6 drops rosewater (optional)

Grind the cardamom with 1 tablespoon water in a pestle and mortar or spice grinder.

Put the almonds, sugar and 250 ml (9 fl oz/1 cup) water in a large, heavy-based saucepan and cook over low heat, stirring constantly until the sugar dissolves. Add the cardamom mixture and stir, removing any scum from the surface. Cook until the syrup thickens. Remove from the heat, strain through a sieve lined with muslin (cheesecloth) and leave to cool.

Add the almond extract and rosewater, if using, and serve in long glasses, with water, over lots of crushed ice.

MAKES 250 ML (9 FL OZ/1 CUP)

PAYASAM

100 g (4 oz/½ cup) sago
2 tablespoons ghee
80 g (3 oz/½ cup) chopped or slivered almonds
125 g (5 oz/1 cup) sultanas
50 g (2 oz) sevian, broken into 3 cm (1¼ in) pieces
1 litre (35 fl oz/4 cups) milk

185 g (7 oz/1 cup) soft brown sugar
3 tablespoons golden syrup
1 teaspoon ground cardamom
¼ teaspoon ground cloves
1 teaspoon rosewater (optional)
2 tablespoons grated coconut (page 243)

Put the sago in a saucepan with 1 litre (35 fl oz/4 cups) water and heat until simmering. Cook, stirring occasionally, for 20–25 minutes, or until the sago is clear, then drain. Rinse and drain the sago again.

Heat the ghee in a heavy-based frying pan over low heat, brown the nuts and sultanas and remove from the pan. Fry the sevian in the same pan until light brown. Add most of the milk and simmer the sevian until soft, stirring as it cooks. Add the sago and remaining milk. Stir with a fork, add the sugar and golden syrup and simmer, stirring constantly.

Add a little milk to the pan if necessary as the payasam thickens, then add the cardamom, cloves and rosewater and stir to a pourable consistency. Add two-thirds of the nuts and sultanas and stir. Serve immediately or chilled, garnished with the coconut and remaining nuts and sultanas.

SERVES 6

TEA

*Tea from China was so important
to Europe by the 18th century that
when trade in tea stopped during the
Opium Wars, the British decided to
grow Chinese tea in India. They then
found a native tea already growing
in Assam.*

The first tea garden in India was established
in 1835 and India quickly became the world's
biggest producer of tea and a nation of tea drinkers.
Tea is made from the leaves of the *Camellia sinensis*
or *Camellia assamica* tree native to both south-west
China and Assam in the far north-east of India.
The leaves can be processed in different ways. Green
tea is dried before fermentation, while black tea is
fermented before drying. In India, black tea (chai)
is the most common.

The process of turning fresh green tea leaves into
black tea is called 'making'. Making tea by either
the CTC or the Orthodox method refers to the
way that the leaves are cut or rolled. CTC means
'crush or cut, tear, curl' – the leaves are fed through

a cutter before they are fermented and dried. This gives a fine, granular tea. Orthodox refers to the method of rolling the leaves (only the best are used) on a rolling table to give whole leaf or broken leaf tea. Both methods break down the veins in the leaves and start the fermentation process. CTC tea is considered to have more strength and Orthodox tea superior flavour. The two are often blended to give a strength and flavour balance.

There are two main tea-producing areas in India, Assam and the Nilgiris. Assam lies beneath the foothills of the Himalayas. Assam tea is produced seasonally in first and second flushes. The second flush produces 'tippy' tea, which means the black tea has plenty of young gold tips. Assam tea is known as 'orange' tea due to its brown and gold colour. Assam teas are full-bodied, with a strong, rich taste which tends to linger in the mouth.

In the Nilgiris, the tea gardens are on the rolling foothills that form part of the Western Ghats in the south of India. Tea produced here has a bright colour and astringent quality and is picked at all times of the year.

Darjeeling, a rich tea produced in the foothills of the Himalayas, has a 'muscatel' flavour. Sometimes described as the champagne of teas, it is produced in limited quantities. Darjeeling tea is often sold as tea from a single garden.

Other areas in India where tea is grown include the Dooars in Bengal, and the Kangara valley in Himachal Pradesh where green tea is produced.

BASICS

An important step in mastering any cuisine is learning the basic recipes and techniques. Straight from the recipe journal, here are the ones no Indian cook would be without.

Panch Phoron

1 teaspoon cumin seeds
1 teaspoon fennel seeds
1 teaspoon fenugreek seeds

1 teaspoon brown mustard seeds
1 teaspoon kalonji (nigella seeds)

Grind all the spices to a fine powder in a spice grinder, a pestle and mortar, or with a grinding stone. Store in a small airtight container until you need it. Use to flavour vegetables and pulses.

MAKES 1 TABLESPOON

Garam Masala

8 cardamom pods
2 Indian bay leaves (cassia leaves)
1 teaspoon black peppercorns
2 teaspoons cumin seeds

2 teaspoons coriander seeds
5 cm (2 in) cinnamon stick
1 teaspoon cloves

Remove the seeds from the cardamom pods and break the bay leaves into small pieces. Put them in a spice grinder or pestle and mortar with the remaining spices and grind to a fine powder. Store in a small airtight container until needed.

MAKES 3 TABLESPOONS

Chaat Masala

4 tablespoons coriander seeds
2 tablespoons cumin seeds
1 teaspoon ajowan
3 tablespoons black salt

1 tablespoon amchoor powder
2 dried chillies
1 teaspoon black peppercorns
1 teaspoon pomegranate seeds

Place a small frying pan over low heat and dry-roast the coriander seeds until aromatic. Remove from the pan and dry-roast the cumin seeds, then separately, the ajowan. Grind the roasted mixture to a fine powder with the other ingredients, using a spice grinder or pestle and mortar. Store in an airtight container. Toss through dry snack mixes or sprinkle onto fruit and vegetables as a seasoning.

PICTURE ON OPPOSITE PAGE

MAKES 10 TABLESPOONS

Rice

Basmati is a fragrant, long-grain rice that gets its unique flavour from the soil in which it is grown. We have cooked it by the absorption method but, if you prefer, you can add the rice to a saucepan of boiling water and boil the rice until ready.

400 g (14 oz/2 cups) basmati rice

Rinse the rice under cold running water until the water running away is clear, then drain well.

Put the rice in a heavy-based saucepan and add enough water to come about 5 cm (2 in) above the surface of the pan. (If you stick your index finger into the rice so it rests on the bottom of the pan, the water will come up to the second joint.) Add

1 teaspoon of salt and bring the water quickly to the boil. When it boils, cover and reduce the heat to a simmer.

Cook for 15 minutes, or until the rice is just tender, then remove the saucepan from the heat and rest the rice for 10 minutes without removing the lid. Fluff the rice with a fork before serving.

SERVES 6

Boiled Rosematter or Patni Rice

Rosematter is eaten in southern India and Patni in central and western India. Both look red and speckled because the rice has been precooked in its husk, leaving some bran and husk stuck to the grain.

400 g (14 oz/2 cups) rosematter or patni rice

Rinse the rice under cold running water until the water running away is clear, then drain well.

Bring a large, heavy-based saucepan of water to the boil and add 1 teaspoon salt. When the water

is at a rolling boil, add the rice and bring back to the boil. Keep at a steady boil for 20 minutes, then test a grain to see if it is cooked. Drain the rice and serve.

SERVES 6

GRATED COCONUT

Grated coconut is best when it is fresh. Dried or desiccated coconut can also be used but it needs to be soaked, then chopped more finely or ground to a paste, otherwise it will be fibrous. If you can buy a proper coconut grater, your life will be much easier.

1 coconut

Drain the coconut by punching a hole in two of the dark, coloured eyes. Drain out the liquid and use it as a refreshing drink. Holding the coconut in one hand, tap around the circumference firmly with a hammer or pestle. This should cause the coconut to split open evenly. If the coconut doesn't crack easily, put it in a 150°C (300°F/Gas 2) oven for 15 minutes. This may cause it to crack as it cools. If it doesn't, it will crack easily when hit with a hammer.

If you would like to use a coconut grater (hiramne), the easiest ones to use are the ones that you sit at one end, then scrape out the coconut from each half on the serrated edge, catching it in a large bowl. If you don't have a coconut grater, prise the flesh out of the shell, trim off the hard, brown, outer skin and grate either by hand on a box grater or chop in a food processor. The grated coconut can be frozen in small portions until it is needed.

MAKES 300 G (11 OZ)

COCONUT MILK AND COCONUT CREAM

Coconut milk is not the liquid that is found inside the coconut, which is the juice or water, but is made by soaking the grated coconut flesh in water and then squeezing it. The first soaking and squeezing gives a thicker milk, sometimes called cream.

1 quantity grated coconut

Mix the grated coconut with 125 ml (4 fl oz/½ cup) hot water and leave to steep for 5 minutes. Pour the mixture through a sieve lined with muslin (cheesecloth), then gather the muslin into a ball to squeeze out any extra liquid. This will make a thick coconut milk.

Repeat the process with another 250 ml (9 fl oz/ 1 cup) water to make thinner coconut milk.

MAKES 125 ML (4 FL OZ/½ CUP) COCONUT CREAM AND 250 ML (9 FL OZ/1 CUP) COCONUT MILK

Paneer

Indian cheese, called paneer or chenna when combined with sugar, is an unripened cheese made by coagulating milk with lemon juice, then leaving it to drain to allow the curds and whey to separate. It is then pressed into blocks.

3 litres (105 fl oz/12 cups) milk
6 tablespoons strained lemon juice, or vinegar

FOR THE CHENNA
1 teaspoon caster (superfine) sugar
1 teaspoon maida or plain (all-purpose) flour

To make the paneer, pour the milk into a large heavy-based saucepan. Bring to the boil, stirring with a wooden spoon so the milk doesn't stick to the base of the pan. Reduce the heat and stir in the lemon juice, then heat over low heat for a few more seconds before turning the heat off as large bits of curd start to form. Shake the pan slowly to allow the curds to form and release the yellow whey. If the curds are slow to form, put the pan over low heat again for a few seconds. This helps with the coagulation.

Line a colander with muslin (cheesecloth) so that it overlaps the sides. Pour off the whey, collecting the curds gently in the colander. Gently pull up the corners of the muslin so that it hangs like a bag, twist the cloth so that the whey is released, then hold the "bag" under running water to wash off the remaining whey, twisting some more to remove the excess liquid.

Leave the bag to hang from a tap for several hours so the weight of the curds releases more liquid and the cheese compacts. To remove some more liquid, press the bag under a heavy weight, such as a tray with some tinned food piled on top, for 1 hour. This will form a firm block of paneer. When the block is firm enough to cut into cubes, the paneer is ready for use.

To make chenna, remove the cheese from the bag and knead the paneer well with the palms of your hands until it is very smooth. Combine the paneer with the sugar and maida, kneading the sugar in until it is fully incorporated.

MAKES 550 G (1 LB 4 OZ)

Tamarind Purée

150 g (6 oz) tamarind block, broken into small pieces

Put the tamarind in a bowl with 250 ml (9 fl oz/ 1 cup) very hot water and soak for 3 hours, or until the tamarind is soft. (If you are in a hurry, you can simmer the tamarind in the water for 15 minutes. Although this is efficient, it doesn't give as good a result.) Mash the tamarind thoroughly with a fork.

Put the mixture through a sieve and extract as much of the pulp as possible by pushing it against the

sieve with the back of a spoon. Put the tamarind in the sieve back in the bowl with another 125 ml (4 fl oz/½ cup) hot water and mash again. Strain again. Discard all of the fibres left in the sieve. The purée can be frozen in 1 tablespoon portions and defrosted as needed.

MAKES 310 ML (11 FL OZ/1¼ CUPS)

Ginger Juice

5 cm (2 in) piece of ginger

Pound the ginger in a pestle and mortar, or grate with a fine grater into a bowl. Put the ginger into

a piece of muslin (cheesecloth), twist it up tightly and squeeze out all the juice.

MAKES 2 TABLESPOONS

Yoghurt

625 ml (22 fl oz/2½ cups) milk

Put the milk in a heavy-based saucepan. Bring to the boil, then cool to lukewarm. Stir in the yoghurt, cover and leave in a warm place for about 8 hours, or overnight. The yoghurt should be thick. If it is too runny, the milk was probably too hot for the starter yoghurt; if it is too milky, the yoghurt was probably not left in a warm enough place to ferment.

2 tablespoons thick plain yoghurt

From each batch, use 2 tablespoons to make the next batch.

When the yoghurt is set, put it in a sieve lined with a piece of muslin (cheesecloth) and leave to drain overnight. This will give a thick yoghurt that does not contain too much moisture.

PICTURE ON OPPOSITE PAGE

MAKES 625 ML (22 FL OZ/2½ CUPS)

GLOSSARY

AGAR-AGAR
Also known as China grass, this is a setting agent made from certain types of seaweed. It is sold as strips, sheets, flakes or powder.

AJOWAN (ajwain)
A spice that looks like miniature cumin seeds and has a similar aroma but stronger flavour.

AMARANTH (marsa)
A leafy green, or green and dark red vegetable. It has a peppery flavour. Substitute with spinach.

AMCHOOR/AMCHUR POWDER (khatai)
A fine powder made by drying green mangoes. It is used as a souring agent or meat tenderizer and is an essential flavour in chaat masala.

ASAFOETIDA (hing)
This yellowish powder or lump of resin is made from the dried latex of a type of fennel. It has an extremely pungent smell which has earned it the name 'devil's dung'. It is used to make pulses and legumes more digestible. Asafoetida is always fried to calm its aroma.

ATTA
Sometimes called chapati flour, this is made from finely ground whole durum wheat. Some have a proportion of white flour added. Atta is much finer and softer than wholemeal flour so if you can't find it, use half wholemeal and half maida or plain (all-purpose) flour.

BANANA FLOWER (kere kafool/mocha)
This is the purple flower of the banana plant. Only the inner pale core is eaten. Wear rubber gloves to prepare banana flower as it has a gummy substance that can stain your fingers.

BANANA LEAVES
Large green leaves which can be used to wrap foods, or as a plate to eat off.

BASIL SEEDS (subja)
These tiny black seeds of a type of wild Indian basil are soaked in water until they swell. When soaked, they are surrounded by clear jelly. They have no flavour and are used for texture.

BESAN FLOUR
Also known as gram flour, this is a yellow flour made from ground Bengal gram or chickpeas. It is used as a thickener in curries, as well as in batters, dumplings, sweets and breads.

BLACK-EYED BEANS (lobhia)
Also called black-eyed peas, these are actually dried cow peas and are also known as chowli dal when split. They are buff-coloured beans with a small dark eye on one side. They need to be soaked overnight or pre-cooked before use.

BLACK SALT (kala namak)
A rock salt mined in central India. It has a tangy, smoky flavour. Available as black or dark brown lumps, or ground to a pinkish-grey powder.

CARDAMOM (elaichi)
Dry green pods full of sticky, tiny brown or black seeds, which have a sweet flavour and pungent aroma. If you need ground cardamom, grind the seeds. Use the pods whole or crushed. Brown cardamom is not suitable for sweet dishes.

CAYENNE PEPPER

A very hot red chilli powder made from sun-dried red chillies.

CHAAT MASALA

Seasoning used for various snacks known as chaat. The spice blend includes asafoetida, amchoor, black salt, cumin, cayenne, ajowan and pepper.

CHANA DAL (gram lentils)

These are husked, split, polished, yellow Bengal gram, the most common type of gram lentil in India. They are often cooked with asafoetida.

CHENNA

Sweetened Indian cheese, used in sweet dishes.

CHICKPEAS (chana)

Chickpeas come white (kabuli/kubli) or black (kala). The white chickpeas are actually tan in colour and the black ones are dark brown. Usually sold whole, but also sold split, dried chickpeas need to be soaked in cold water for 8 hours.

CHILLI POWDER

A wide variety of chillies are dried and crushed to make chilli powders. Some, such as Kashmiri chilli powder and paprika, are used for colour, whereas others like cayenne are used for heat.

CHILLIES (lal mirch/hari mirch)

Red and green chillies are widely used in Indian cuisine. Recipes generally give a colour, rather than a variety. Many varieties are grown in India and are used in a regional or seasonal context.

CLOVES (laung)

The dried, unopened flower buds of the clove tree. Brown and nail-shaped, they have a pungent flavour, so use in moderation.

COCONUT (nariyal)

The fruit of a coconut palm. The inner nut is encased in a husk that has to be removed. The hard shell can then be drained of juice and cracked open to extract the white meat.

COCONUT CREAM

This is made by soaking freshly grated coconut in boiling water and then squeezing out a thick, sweet coconut-flavoured liquid.

COCONUT MILK

A thinner version of coconut cream, made with more water or from a second pressing.

COCONUT MILK POWDER

A powdered form of coconut which when mixed with water makes coconut milk or cream.

CORIANDER (hara dhaniya)

Fresh coriander (cilantro) leaves are used in recipes and as a colourful garnish.

CORIANDER (dhaniya) SEEDS

The seeds of the coriander plant. They have a spicy aroma, are widely used in Indian cooking and are common in spice mixes such as garam masala. To intensify the flavour, dry-roast the seeds until aromatic, before crushing them.

CREAMED COCONUT

A solid block of coconut cream which needs to be reconstituted with water, or can be added straight to a dish to give a strong coconut flavour. Slice pieces off the block as required.

CUMIN (jeera) SEEDS

The green or ochre, elongated seeds of a plant of the parsley family. It has a peppery, slightly bitter flavour and is very aromatic. To intensify the flavour, dry-roast the seeds before crushing.

CURRY LEAVES (kadhi patta/meetha neem)

Smallish green aromatic leaves of a tree native to India and Sri Lanka. These give a distinctive flavour to south Indian dishes. They are usually fried and added to the dish or used as a garnish.

DAL (dhal)

Used to describe not only an ingredient but a dish made from it. In India, dal relates to any type of dried split pea, bean or lentil. Cooking times vary as do the texture and flavour. A dal dish can be a thin soup or more like a stew. All dal should be rinsed before use.

FENNEL (saunph) SEEDS
The dried seeds of a Mediterranean plant, fennel seeds look like large cumin and are used as an aromatic and a digestive. To intensify the flavour, dry-roast the seeds before crushing.

FENUGREEK (methi) SEEDS
Not a true seed, but a dried legume. Ochre in colour and almost square, fenugreek has a curry aroma (it is a major ingredient in commercial curry powders) and is best dry-roasted for a few seconds before use. Don't brown the seeds too much or they will be bitter.

GARAM MASALA
Meaning 'warming spice mix', garam masala is a northern Indian spice mix. It mostly contains coriander, cumin, cardamom, black pepper, cloves, cinnamon and nutmeg. Garam masala is usually added to meat dishes as a final seasoning.

GHEE
A highly clarified butter made from cow or water buffalo milk. Ghee has an aromatic flavour and can be heated to a high temperature without burning. You can substitute clarified butter.

GINGER (adrak)
The rhizome of a tropical plant. Fresh ginger should have a smooth, pinkish beige skin and be firm and juicy. As it ages, the skin toughens and the flesh becomes more fibrous. Avoid old ginger that is wrinkled as it will be tough. Ginger is also available dried and ground.

GREEN UNRIPE MANGO (kacha am)
A variety of mango widely used for cooking in Asian countries.

HILSA (elish)
A much-prized fish, this is a type of shad with sweet flesh and lots of tiny bones. Large herrings or firm white fish can be used instead.

INDIAN BAY LEAVES (tej patta)
These are the dried leaves of the cassia tree. They look somewhat like European bay leaves but have a cinnamon flavour. They are used mainly in Bengali cuisine and cuisine of the north of India.

JAGGERY (gur)
Made from sugar cane, this is a raw sugar with a caramel flavour and alcoholic aroma. It is sold in lumps, is slightly sticky and varies in colour depending on the juice from which it is made. Jaggery can also refer to palm sugar. Soft brown sugar can be used as a substitute.

KALONJI (nigella seeds)
Small teardrop-shaped black seeds with an onion flavour, used as a spice in northern India and as a decoration for breads such as naan. It is used in panch phoron.

KARHAI/KADHAI
A deep wok-shaped cooking dish. Heavy cast iron ones are best for talawa (deep-frying) and carbon steel ones for bhoona (frying).

KASHMIRI CHILLI POWDER
Made from ground red Kashmiri chillies, which have a deep red colour but little heat. A mild, dark red chilli powder can be substituted.

KOKUM
The dried purple fruit of the gamboge tree which is used in southern Indian, Gujarati and Maharashtran cuisine to impart an acid fruity flavour. Kokum looks like dried pieces of purple/black rind and is quite sticky. It needs to be briefly soaked before use.

MAIDA
Plain white flour used for making naan and other Indian recipes. Plain (all-purpose) flour is a suitable substitute.

MASOOR DAL (red lentils)
When whole these are brown or green. When split, they are salmon in colour. The split ones are the most common as they cook more easily.

METHI (fenugreek leaves)
The leaves of young fenugreek plants, these are used as a vegetable, much like spinach. They have a mildly bitter flavour. Strip the leaves off the stalks as the stalks are often tough.

MOONG DAL
Split and skinned mung beans, which are pale yellow. The dal does not always need to be soaked. Whole mung beans (sabat moong), also called green gram, must be soaked before use.

MUSTARD OIL (sarson ka tel)
Made from pressed brown mustard seeds, this is a strongly flavoured oil used in Bengali and Punjabi cooking. It is usually heated to smoking point and then cooled to temper its aroma.

MUSTARD SEEDS (rai)
Yellow, brown and black mustard seeds are used in Indian cooking, especially in Bengal. Brown and black are interchangeable. The seeds are either added to hot oil to pop, to make them taste nutty rather than hot, or ground to a paste. Split mustard seeds are called mustard dal.

OIL (tel)
Several types of oil are used in Indian cuisine. Cold-pressed or refined peanut (groundnut) oil is used in northern and central India and is a good all-purpose oil (use only the refined version for deep-frying). Sesame oil made from raw sesame seeds is used in the South, and mustard oil in the Punjab and Bengal. Coconut oil is also used in the South.

OKRA (bhindi)
Also known as ladies' fingers, these are green, fuzzy, tapered pods with ridges running down them. When cut they give off a mucilaginous substance which disappears during cooking.

PANCH PHORON (panch phora)
Meaning five spices, this mix contains fennel, brown mustard, kalonji, fenugreek, and cumin seeds in equal amounts. Use whole or ground.

PANEER
A fresh cheese made by coagulating milk with lemon juice and leaving it to drain. Paneer is usually pressed into a block.

PAPRIKA (deghi mirch)
A reddish orange powder made from ground capsicums (peppers) grown in Kashmir. Usually sweet rather than hot, paprika is used for colour.

POMEGRANATE SEEDS (anardana)
Sun-dried whole or ground sour pomegranate seeds, used to add a sour, tangy flavour to north Indian dishes. They are also used as a garnish.

POMFRET (rupchanda, chamna)
A silvery seawater fish with tiny black spots. Pomfret is expensive and hard to find outside India. Sole, flounder, leatherjacket or John Dory fillets can be substituted.

POPPADOM (papadam, papad, appalam)
These are thin wafers made from a paste of lentil (gram) flours, rice flour or even tapioca or sago flour, which is rolled out and then sun-dried.

POPPY SEEDS (khus khus)
In India, white poppy seeds are used rather than the European black or grey ones. Ground poppy seeds are used to thicken dishes. Whole ones are often used in spice mixes.

PUFFED RICE (moori, mamra, kurmura)
Puffed rice is made by exploding dried rice out of its husks by dropping the grains onto hot sand. It is used in snacks such as bhel puri, or rolled in jaggery to make sweets.

RICE (chaaval)
Rice grain types and sizes vary across India. Much of the rice which is eaten is grown locally and it is nearly always white and polished.

RICE FLOUR (chaaval ka atta)
Finely ground rice that is used for making dosas. A coarser grind called idli-rava is used for idlis.

ROASTED CHANA DAL
Bengal gram which have been roasted so they puff up and get a porous, crunchy texture.

ROHU
A black, silvery carp with one central bone and firm flesh. Any firm-fleshed fish can be used.

ROSEWATER (ruh gulab/gulab jal)
Made from rose essence and water, this is used to perfume sweets, desserts and drinks. It has aroma but no flavour. Use sparingly.

SAFFRON STRANDS (kesar/zaffran)
The dried stigmas of a crocus flower. The strands give an intense yellow colour and musky aroma. Indian saffron grows in Kashmir.

SAGO (sabudhana)
Small dried balls of sago palm sap that are used for milky desserts and savoury dishes. Cooked sago is transparent and soft with a silky texture.

SEMOLINA (sooj, rava)
A fine, coarse or medium grain made from processed wheat with the wheat germ removed. It swells when cooked to give a creamy, textured effect. Used for sweets and upama.

SEV
Very fine noodles, used in bhel puri, made from besan flour.

SEVIAN
These are very fine noodles made from wheat flour. They have a biscuity flavour.

SILVER LEAF (varak)
Very thin, edible sheets of silver. They have no flavour or aroma and come in boxes or books between sheets of tissue paper. Always apply the silver to the food from the backing sheet.

SPLIT PEAS (matar dal)
Split dried peas which need to be soaked before they are cooked and have a slightly chewy texture. Green and yellow ones are available.

TAMARIND (imli)
A souring agent made from the pods of the tamarind tree. Sold either as a block of pulp, fibrous husk and seeds, as cleaned pulp, or as ready-prepared tamarind purée or concentrate.

TARKA
A seasoning process, either the first or last step, used in Indian cookery. Spices and aromatics are fried in oil to flavour the oil, then the oil is stirred into the dish.

TAVA
A specially shaped hotplate used in India to cook breads. Either flat, slightly convex or concave.

TOOR DAL (toovar dal)
Also called yellow lentils, these come oiled and plain. Oiled ones look slightly greasy and need to be soaked in hot water to remove the oil.

TURMERIC (haldi)
Dried turmeric is a deep yellow colour. It has a slightly bitter flavour and a pungent aroma.

URAD DAL
The split variety (chilke urad) is a cream colour with black skin. The skinned variety is cream. Urad dal does not usually need to be soaked. The dal is used in dosa and idli batters and it becomes glutinous and creamy when cooked.

VINEGAR (sirka)
Made from fermented alcohol, vinegars based on sugar cane molasses (dark) and coconut (clear) are used. If unavailable, substitute balsamic or white vinegar.

WHOLE BLACK GRAM (sabat urad)
This whole urad dal has a black skin. Usually it has to be soaked or precooked before use.

YOGHURT (dahi, doi)
Yoghurt in India is made with whole milk and is a thick, set yoghurt. If you use commercial yoghurt, drain it in muslin (cheesecloth) first to remove any excess liquid.

INDEX

❀❀❀❀❀❀❀❀❀❀❀❀❀❀❀❀❀❀❀❀❀❀❀❀❀❀❀❀❀❀❀❀❀❀

Published in 2010 by Murdoch Books Pty Limited

Murdoch Books Australia
Pier 8/9, 23 Hickson Road
Millers Point NSW 2000
Phone: +61 (0) 2 8220 2000
Fax: +61 (0) 2 8220 2558
www.murdochbooks.com.au

Murdoch Books UK Limited
Erico House, 6th Floor
93–99 Upper Richmond Road
Putney, London SW15 2TG
Phone: +44 (0) 20 8785 5995
Fax: +44 (0) 20 8785 5985
www.murdochbooks.co.uk

Chief Executive: Juliet Rogers
Publishing Director: Kay Scarlett

Publisher: Lynn Lewis
Senior Designer: Heather Menzies
Series Design Concept and Design: Sarah Odgers
Project Manager: Justine Harding
Editorial Coordinator: Liz Malcolm
Production: Joan Beal
Photographer: Jason Lowe (location); Alan Benson (recipes)
Index: Jo Rudd

National Library of Australia Cataloguing-in-Publication Data:
Title: India.
ISBN: 978-1-74196-438-7 (pbk.)
Series: World Kitchen.
Notes: Includes index.
Subjects: Cookery, Indian.
Dewey Number: 641.5954

A catalogue record for this book is available from the British Library.

PRINTED IN CHINA